<u>Caught In Between</u>
Thoughts and Musings on the Spiritual life

By Stephen Pate

Cover design by Paul Wallace

For Unkie

The Content

Act I: Earth Bound

Act II: Seeing Beyond

Act III: Echoes of Heaven

ACT I Earth Bound

"There are two ways to live. One is as though nothing is a miracle. The other is as though everything is a miracle." *Albert Einstein*

"Then Moses said, 'Now show me your glory.'" Exodus 33:18

The journey of living life caught *in between* begins here. It is in us, intrinsically attached to our lives—eating and drinking and kissing and growing up. Our stories up until now have been revealing this truth to us: Earth is crammed with Heaven.

Homesick For a Place We've Never Been

No matter what you think about God, faith, church or religion, have you ever wondered if there is more to life than what you see? I'm not looking for logical or scientific answers, but imagination. Outside of the definable and definitive, beyond the measurable and knowable, have you wandered like a curious child into regions of intrigue? Have you looked up at a tall tree and not seen a tree, but a thousand year old sage full to the brim of stories from a lifetime ago?

I've always looked at life through a lens of fantasy and make believe, of story and fable. Throughout the years, my life appeared to be a shadow of something greater to come. Perhaps I'm just the product of being an only child for the first nine years of my life who spent his free time creating playmates out of inanimate objects and visions from my head. Perhaps I spent a lot of time alone when I was young. I'm not really sure. Whatever the reason, I spent an inordinate amount of my time with my head in the clouds.

I can remember sitting underneath the lemon trees in my grandma's backyard in Pomona, staring up at the sky, wondering if someone or something would send a sign. My grandma had a huge plot of land, right next to the 60 freeway. Part of her property was reserved for her massive garden. Tulips, lilies, and daffodils spread in all directions like her very own Garden of Eden. A long driveway sloped the outside of the garden, leading to the back of the property that was one big golden field. My grandma didn't water this part of the lawn, so it was a giant stretch of yellow grass and an apricot tree. I used to sit underneath that tree just to watch the clouds roll by.

I think those summer days under the shade of the apricot tree influenced my faith as much as any sermon or Bible study. Growing up, I heard people talk about hearing from God, like there was a direct connection from Heaven to Earth and God yelled down at us on His one-way line. I spent time trying to hear from Him, too. I'd sit idly by for a few minutes, close my eyes, and strain my ears, just waiting for some sort of sign. Anything would do. One time I swore I heard a voice. It was late in October when the leaves begin to change colors. It was cold and the first rain since early summer came pouring down. I walked home from school with the wind howling around me, and I thought I felt God in the wind, His Spirit whispering in my ears.

Growing up, I observed my friends and family living for the chase—caught in ephemeral pursuits of pleasure and success. I followed in suit—education, love, and money, grasping for anything I could hold onto. None of it mattered though or made much sense. The only constant thing in my life has been the person of Jesus Christ. I'm not here to talk about religion or politics, or even issues of morality. Someone else can do that. I just want to talk about Jesus and the life He offers.

See, I grew up going to church. I know a lot of people share the same experience. More often than not, it seems growing up in church usually messes someone up. They get force-fed content from a young age and eventually turn away from faith. I know it happens, and it makes sense. My experience, though, was different. I've always been a person with a lot of questions about God and someone who is prone to doubt (I think most of us are). There are things in the Bible that are hard to understand. I question, doubt, and get angry quite often. But something keeps bringing me back—back to Jesus and His poetic words and visionary life.

The life of Jesus as told by His earliest followers is the most captivating account of a person's life I've ever heard. It's the way He lived and the way He loved. It's the life He didn't guard but gave away freely. I'm convinced now more than ever that the way to a full, beautiful life is found in Him. Even when things around me don't make sense, He does. And that's why I keep coming back.

This is a story about the Jesus I'm coming to know. His words are kind, and His presence warm. He is patient. Love is His motivation. We are recipients of the grandest gesture of all time—Himself. This is the aspect of faith that I am motivated to pursue: Faith that isn't based on an idea or set of principles, but faith that is attached to a figure that is worth emulating.

Jesus reminds us it is a gift to be human. Truly. We are living in tension. Beautiful tension that reminds us this world is not our true home. We are from another place. The gift of being human is the realization that we are caught *in between*. We exist in a space that reminds us of our strength and also our frailty. Like nomad wanderers we are on our way, with much of the journey left before us. There are traces of our true home along the way, and every day we are getting closer to what we know is real.

The ancient Greeks believed humanity was experiencing this enormous tension of being caught between Heaven and Earth. They believed they were created for more than this life, and yet this earth was their home. Grounded here to toil the earth, but all the while searching the heavens for answers.

The Greeks understood something quite profound: the tension of being caught in between. Deep down inside, we are all fighting this, aren't we? We are wrestling with the middle. We know there is more to life than what we see here. The Earth is crying out to show us how close Heaven is, and Heaven is beckoning us to leave the temporariness of this world behind. Jesus spoke about Heaven and Earth one day forming into one existence. He spoke about the time when all things would be made new. Until that point, however, we are simply in limbo between this world and the next. We are living stories that remind us of the brokenness of the world and the awesomeness of Heaven.

Perhaps a compelling definition of the church would be a gathering of people homesick for a place they've never been. This band of brothers and sisters is united by hope for a better world and a purer existence. Hope in our Lord, that there is more to this life than what we see. Belief that Heaven is coming down and we are part of creation's redemption. Having been given keys to the kingdom, we are stumbling towards its doors.

Those in the church live life in the middle. We are caught in between the glory of Heaven and the brokenness of the world. And, yet, we are finding the two are closer than we know. It's a gift to be a human. It's a glorious life to live in the tension, to know earth is not our final home. I'm learning more and more, it is a gift it is to be caught in between.

This book is a collection of stories focused on seeing our lives in the coming but not yet, beautiful but tragic, uproarious yet somber, journey of *life in between.*

The Art of Dreaming

I used to think God's sole purpose was to reveal the unknowable. Now I'm convinced His genius lies in helping us discover what we've known all along.

A little more about me…

When I was eight years old, my mother and I moved from Southern California to the great northwest city of Portland, Oregon. I don't remember much from those early days other than one Christmas we had sunshine and blue skies, and the next Christmas was cloudy and rainy and cold and people wore copious amounts of flannel and socks with sandals.

My mother, wanting the best education she could for me, enrolled me in Catholic Parochial School. Thus began an eight-year relationship with Holy Cross Elementary School.

For the first eight years of my educated life, I was confused. I was learning a lot about faith from many different angles and it was difficult to reconcile it all. I attended a Protestant church on Sunday with my family and mass on Wednesdays with my school. Eat your heart out, Martin Luther. I towed the line.

I didn't go through confirmation like the other kids in my class or receive my First Communion in the first grade. I just kind of went along with everything as a bystander who was a part of it, but not. A perennial wallflower to the Catholic faith. I remember sitting in Mass one Wednesday morning, listening to the gospel presented by the priest. I wondered if I had what it took to become a priest and speak in front of a congregation. I imagined God opening the roof of the church and smiling down favorably at the priest who was busy saying this and that, but scowling at me. He would scowl because he knew I really wasn't paying attention.

For the Wednesday morning masses, a class would be put in charge to handle details in the service. We'd make a banner, walk down the aisle in a grand processional, and then we were given different roles to play. I was often jealous because my friends in school were allowed to be altar boys, but I could only participate in the less structured activities. The closest I got was playing in our fifth grade recorder ensemble, which I'm sure was absolutely riveting to the audience. We stood up and blew the notes out during the opening processional. I remember trying so hard to learn the Simpson's theme song in music class that I couldn't actually play the song we were supposed to learn. I think it was Ave Maria. Our music teacher shot disappointed glances our way for the myriad of sharp and flat notes.

The same year that I blew out pitchy notes on the recorder, my teacher, Sister Ruth Frank, gave us an assignment I found thrilling. We were asked to invent something and then present that invention to the class. I got excited about this venture and did my best to come up with what I believed was a truly creative idea. In hindsight, you could tell what kids had their parents do their assignment for them— let's be honest, there's no way the kid who ate paste in first grade came up with a self-cleaning oven rack. Anyway, my invention was something I called "The Radio Bike." Get this: it was a bike, with a radio on it. I thought it was fantastic for some reason. My teacher told me someone already invented it, so it wasn't really an invention. My dreams were crushed.

Even though my invention didn't pan out, and I didn't have much to offer during the weekly mass, I can remember the most redemptive part of my education—the thirty minutes of recess after lunch. Regardless of what happened during class, recess was where we dreamed. We were NBA players taking audacious shots as the clock ran down; we were NFL superstars lobbing Hail Mary passes (no pun intended) into an end zone that was deep and wide. There was even a rambunctious game of kick ball where everyone in our class participated, no matter their level of skill. Recess was the constant reminder that life was bigger than the moment, and there was more to come then what had been. It reminded even the most apprehensive grade school student that dreams are real.

Dreams are powerful. They have the potential to make us soar; they give our lives meaning and the courage to do the impossible. Dreams are fodder for the fire of life, making us move from the present into the future. But dreams are easier when you're a grade school student contemplating the great beyond of primary school. As we grow older, it seems, dreams become harder to realize. They're like a fog that slowly dissipates.

I wonder if there's been a moment in your life where you realized you weren't dreaming anymore? You took a survey of your life, and it hit you: you aren't where you thought you'd be at this point in time. You begin to think that you lost something that was so precious years ago—when you were younger and freer, and your dreams seemed so real. I had a moment like that a few years ago. I was watching American Idol with a few high school students from my church. One of the contestants was 24. I was 24 at the time, and one of my students said, "Wow, look what he's done at 24." She turned to me and said, "You must feel bad, huh?"

At that moment I released the attack dogs.

Okay, I didn't. But it made me think: Where is my life heading? Do I know who I am and where I want to be? I see a lot of people who have no idea who they want to be. They may have dreams of making a lot of money and falling in love, but their life is one vacuous shell lacking substance. They feel empty. It's sort of like that overly used *Brave Heart* quote that I will now insert here unabashedly: "Every man dies, but not every man lives."[1] Most of us are still figuring out how to live. We see images of the good life and hear rumors that another way is possible, but at the end of the day, we are stuck in our ongoing battle of monotony and boredom.

A few years ago, I met a lady named Florence who works for a non-profit organization in Nairobi, Kenya. I was at a conference where she was discussing what her organization does and how people in The States can partner with them to help people living thousands of miles away. Someone in the crowd asked a question about the AIDS epidemic. Florence responded by talking about how life in the slums of Kiberra—one of the largest slums in the world—is a huge challenge to survive. She talked about how AIDS has spread so quickly because sometimes people who are not romantically involved end up having sex. Then she said something interesting: A lot of people are having sex in the slums where she works because they're bored. *Sex because they're bored?* AIDS is spreading at an alarming rate and sometimes the reason is because of *boredom?*

I have the feeling that a lot of us, whether we'd like to admit it or not, are just plain bored. The American Dream of our grandparents was to have kids, own property and have a car in the driveway. It was family oriented and simple. Things have changed though. No longer are we satisfied with the pursuit of that archaic 1950s pipe-dream. We want something more. Our souls are crying out in a world that has been selling us this newer version of the same dream—nicely packaged and wrapped up for years—and finally we've mustered up the courage to revolt against it. It's like we want it all, but we want nothing to do with it at the same time.

I thought about this the other day when listening to a Katy Perry song on the radio. The song is called "Teenage Dream."[2] The dream, as described by the song, is to behold someone you love and pursue him recklessly like a teenager who doesn't think about the future, but only lives in the present. I think the reason the song resonates so well with our culture is that most of us wish we could return to that innocent, teen-like state where the world was ours. We've realized over the years that the dream we were pursuing didn't satisfy us, nor did it bring the fulfillment we thought it would. We wanted our lives to count for something, and now have the shocking and somewhat inconvenient truth that our dreams didn't pan out the way we wanted.

And for this reason, we've stopped dreaming. It wasn't that the act of dreaming was too idealistic, wrong, or even misguided.

Rather, it was the blatant truth that the dreams we had were based on a lie. Our soul could never be satisfied or won over by the promises of stuff, pleasure, or achievement. These types of pursuits are never really satisfying. We always want more and yearn for the next best thing. The thrill and adrenaline we receive from our "achievements" keeps coming back for more like chronic arthritis in our bones—it never truly goes away.

What's more, we tend to know all of this, and yet we can't do anything to curb it. It's the ugly, over-sized elephant in the corner of the room taking up more space than we'd like to admit. All of our hopes of making it big and being a star come crashing down. And the result? We are left defeated, jaded, and quite frankly, bored.

My best friend, Kyle, is the kind of guy who's been dreaming for a number of years. He knows his time on this earth is limited, and he wants to do his best to leave behind a legacy for those who follow after him. One of the ways he's started doing this is by making a list in a notebook of his favorite books. He calls these his "Gold-Star" collection and, yes, they really do have a gold star on them. These are the books he is leaving behind for his children, and in case anything were to ever happen to him, they would have this notebook of his thoughts and a collection of his favorite books. In that way, they would know their dad pretty well.

A couple years ago, Kyle had a quarter life-crisis. He turned thirty. This is great for a number of reasons, but he started feeling sort of old. Now that he's thirty, he is pretty much set in his ways for a while. He's gone through his twenties and picked a wife, found a career, and now he has a kid. Not that thirty is old by any stretch of the imagination, but it does signal a transition. By this point, your college days are well behind you, and you start thinking differently about how you spend and invest your time. Things like life insurance and your kid's preschool start to become actual conversation topics. Kyle reckons it to the "End of an Era." I get it because I recently experienced the same thing. But the end of one thing is really just the beginning of something new.

That is the pattern of life. There are moments when life seems ephemeral and chaotic, and things are over as soon as they begin. Other times, we tend to move gradually, almost as if life were moving in slow motion, and time is on our side.

I had one of those life-altering seasons of life a few years back. It was one summer that made me rethink everything. In hindsight, it was one of greatest periods of growth in my life. I remember that before the summer started, a pastor I was working for gave me a journal with the instruction to simply "write stuff." That was it—just write stuff. So, for an entire summer, I jotted down my thoughts, frustrations, feelings, and dreams. I filled the pages with my anguish and joy. I took the advice of Hemingway, and I sat down at my open page and just allowed myself to bleed.

This summer of writing revealed a longing deep inside me. It was the famous French philosopher Blaise Pascal who said this longing is a "God-shaped hole."[3] According to Pascal, somewhere deep down inside all of us, there is a longing for something more than what we're living for that can only be filled by finding God. Sure, we can attempt to fill the void with everything under the sun, but the gap will never truly be closed. Not by our own doing.

Inside our dreams and hopes, our losses and setbacks, God is calling out to us. He's put that longing in us and invites us to pursue it. When most of us think about God pursuing us or calling out to us, our initial response is He must be angry or upset or pointing out our failures. But what if He wasn't? What if, instead, He was trying to show us something? What if He cares so deeply about us that He's guiding us towards a better life—something not based on the dreams of our culture, but rooted in the love of our Creator? What if this "other" way of living was an exciting life that took us on an adventure we'd never forget. Rather than experience monotony and boredom, we find originality and a new zest for life. What if it meant we went to the best parties, drank deep from the fountain of life, and found inspiration everywhere?

What if we could stop the rat race of American consumerism and success and find something truly worth our time and money? And what if we started to experience this "life to the full" that Jesus speaks about in the Scriptures? What if following Jesus is an invitation to dream in a way we never have before?

I spent a few months in Kenya in the summer of 2006. After landing in Nairobi, I boarded a bus from the airport to travel out to the country. Everything looked like it was right out of a movie. I was on the set of the *Ghost in the Darkness*, or *The Lion King*. But those images changed quickly. After only a few days in Kenya, I attended a funeral for a young girl who died of AIDS. At first, I didn't think the funeral could be real. The casket was so small. Family and friends gathered around this small casket, saying prayers and remembering this beautiful life. I felt like an imposter at the funeral, not knowing why I was there other than my hosts took me with them.

The next day we picked up a girl named Judy. She was the older sister of the girl who passed away and whose funeral we attended days earlier. Our job was to transport her to school, which happened to be on the top of a mountain a few miles away. We made a stop in town to pick up some school supplies for her. It was here in town, on a busy street corner, that she was told of her younger sister's death. I was told what was happening, and I stood on the street corner next to Judy as she sobbed quietly on hearing about the death of her sister for the first time. Then it was just the two of us. I stood there praying for Judy, not knowing what to say or do.

Judy wiped the tears from her eyes and looked up at me. "I'm going to finish school and become a doctor," she said. "Then I will work hard to find a cure for AIDS." In that moment, our eyes locked, but it was as if our souls were communicating. I can't shake the memory of Judy and me on that busy street corner, looking together at a future that was possible and open; it was a dream so powerful and contagious it could not be stopped. I've never met anyone who looked more determined than Judy in that moment. Moreover, I haven't heard of a more beautiful dream.

Dreams focused on and fueled by something greater than ourselves change the world. That's a true statement. And it's one God backs up.

There's a section of the Scriptures in the Old Testament known as the minor prophets. These individuals were courageous spokesmen who held nothing back, crying out for change, justice, and a better future. One of these prophets named Joel prophesied that visions and dreams would become apparent in the last days. The phrase the "Last Days" in the Bible is symbolic of a new age and a new existence. Joel was saying there would come a time when people of all ages and backgrounds would share in this venture.

This same prophetic statement is echoed in the book of Acts during the birth of the church.[4] When Jesus creates this gathering of men and women, the passage of Joel is quoted, and we learn that Joel was actually talking about us. The church, it appears, is this new time for dreamers to unite together fueled by God's creative visions.

God needs dreamers—men and women homesick for a place they've never been and who long to see heaven on earth. Dreams are the connecting piece that reminds us we are from a different place. Our wildest dreams make sense when they're founded in the adventurous life of Jesus.

The invitation to each and every one of us is to partner with God in dreaming big, audacious dreams. His call is for us to be caught in something bigger than ourselves. The pulse of heaven is men and women who understand life is about more than what we see—the realization there is more going on around us than what we sense physically.

The first step of living *in between* is to begin dreaming. We may get older and wiser, but we never stop dreaming. Dreams are the bridge of this life to the next, an invitation to re-imagine the world in all its beauty and intrigue.

Why Growing Up Is All the Rage

I used to think growing older meant losing part of your soul. When we look at the life of Jesus, though, there's something redemptive about growing up. Turns out, it's possible to get older and younger at the same time.

There is a change that happens somewhere in your late twenties. I'm not sure how else to say it, but you receive an epiphany of sorts. You figure out you're no longer eighteen. Something has happened in you. You can't keep living your life as if you're not grown. I remember what it was like for me. It was an incredible realization, but it also hurt. I was no longer a kid. I was out of my infantile state and it was time for me to grow up.

I don't think we give enough credit to ourselves during adolescence. I think we forget that growing up is hard. It's difficult to live in this world when we're trying to find ourselves. I've often wondered what God thinks about the whole process of growing up. Does He see our struggles? Does He understand the pain of losing what we want? Does He get what it's like to be broken? I think He does.

I remember being a young, spry eighteen year-old with my eyes full of hope and life. I believed there was nothing in this world that could stop me or slow me down. In hindsight, I'm not sure if I'd call that confidence or naivety. Maybe it was a bit of both. At eighteen, I was searching for something. I wanted more than what was in front of me, but I was too young to understand the complications of everything I longed for.

It's kind of like what happened in the book *The Perks of Being a Wallflower.*[5] The protagonist of the story, Charlie, is in high school with the world at his fingertips, and he's desperately attempting to sort things out. And it hurts. When you read the book, you are taken to a place of time gone by where you feel the pain too. Adolescence is no joke. Love hurts. Broken friendships ache. Unfulfilled dreams drain you. No one ever tells you that this life is going to come with undesired stuff. No one ever tells you part of growing up is living and existing in brokenness.

We've all had those moments where happiness and sadness exist concurrently. At times, we have been happy to be where we are, but simultaneously, we also have been sad to know it wasn't going to last. We find ourselves searching for the next thing, for the next part of the journey. I think this is part of what it means to grow up. We learn to live with the happiness and sadness together, like they are dance partners. We learn that feelings are just feelings— emotions that neither control us nor define us. And we learn life, unlike stories, doesn't always resolve.

Getting older doesn't make living this life easier. It does, however, provide us with insight. The older we get, the more in tune we are with what really matters. I believe that. But there is still a chance we are going to miss it. Entirely. We miss it because we are stuck in sadness. Our brokenness comes up again and hits us where it hurts. I know it does for me.

We are only fooling ourselves. Life is not about *getting it* or *finding it.* There isn't some magic place we come to where we figure out everything that eluded us earlier. It just doesn't work like that. This journey is difficult for a reason. It's difficult because to be mature and well-adjusted people, we have to go through fire. And even as adults, we are still going through it.

We're not finished yet.

This isn't the final product.

We are still works in progress.

We haven't arrived yet, but maybe we are closer than we were before.

Your life may not be exactly where you wanted it to be at this point. Don't worry—you're not alone. Part of our journey of growing older is learning to strive forward even in the midst of uncertainty. We might not have it all figured out, but we have something necessary for change. We have discontent. And discontentment is the first step to changing who you are. It is a tiny voice beckoning us to be different.

Growing up is hard because getting older hurts. We hear the small voice inviting us to something more, to have something better, and we choose how to respond. This life is all about choices and we get to choose who we are everyday. Even if you didn't like who you were yesterday, yesterday is gone. We have today and that is as good a reason as any to change. Just as the river keeps on turning downstream, we allow our lives to shift and change as well. I want to keep moving forward, focused on what is important. But I'm so incredibly scared. Scared I'm going to mess this up. Because growing up is hard.

Faith, like growing up, is a process. It doesn't just happen overnight. Time must have its way for faith to grow and mature. It needs to be refined over the years. I might still have similar struggles as I did when I was younger, but my faith is different now. I still doubt, struggle, wonder, and ache in my soul. But there is a calm confidence I now possess. There is something I hang onto when the storm comes. And no matter how strong the wind blows, or how high the waves crash upon me, I know I'm not going to drown. As the writer in Hebrews says, "We have this hope as an anchor for the soul, firm and secure."[6] There is an anchor holding me tight. That, to me, is what growing up in your faith is all about—you learn to navigate the storm, even if you don't want to.

Last year I got to hang out with a few pastors over lunch at a gathering of local area ministers. These men are ministry veterans, each putting in around twenty years or so, which is pretty amazing in and of itself. I asked them about their thoughts and feelings toward ministry. I wondered if there were still moments where they wanted to quit. Did they still feel overwhelmed or angry or upset? Did they ever want to rip their name placard off their office door, get in their car, and drive away into the sunset? These were honestly the thoughts I had because I think this way at times. That sounds drastic, but ask anyone in ministry if they feel the same. It comes with the territory.

Anyway, these ministry veterans answered me candidly. There was a collective sigh, then a unanimous answer that came from every single one of them. Turns out, they still feel that urge to quit. They still deal with low self-esteem, anger, frustration, and the stress of ministry. But something in them has developed over the years. Maybe you can call it thick skin or a depth of commitment. I'm not sure at this point how to describe it, but they told me that even in the dark days, nothing can take them from their callings. This keeps them moving forward, no matter what.

If there was one take away I took from their responses, I'd say they've learned to grow up. They've gained an entirely new perspective that doesn't come from classes or seminaries or books or podcasts, but from experience.

We need to see our lives for what they are. We've been invited to be part of an adventure—an adventure in growing up in Jesus.

A life of following Jesus is utter and complete madness. There's really no other way to accurately describe the life He invites His followers to live. He calls us to abandon ourselves in favor of His ways. He calls us to choose sacrifice and humility, to choose love in all things. It's a crazy journey going from here to there. Life is not dull or monotonous, but it is an experience of beautiful freedom and intrigue. I often think about what happens next as a direct result of where I'm willing to go. What adventures am I willing to have?

God invites us to a life of adventure, to a life of seeing where the road takes us. There is a partnership in mind that God provides. He has laid the road down in front of us, but we choose which direction to take it. Anyone who believes God is guiding them down a certain, fixed path, is someone who has misunderstood Scripture. God is not a puppet king, only allowing us to travel a certain journey. No, He has given us freedom and free will to figure out things on our own way. It's as if Heaven is leaning on the rails to see what we'll do next.

I like thinking of my life like that. There is a sense of freedom in knowing that what happens next is largely up to me. Life is an unchartered adventure, and I choose what adventure to take myself on.

It's kind of funny to think about growing up. Things happened in our past and choices were made that directly correlate with the present. Small, somewhat inconsequential events have even played a role in our current stories. Our parents decisions to move to a certain part of the country, or even to live in a certain neighborhood determined where we went to school and maybe even the friends we grew up having. In some ways, our parents experiences have transferred to us.

My aunt tells this story about my dad growing up. When they were little, they used to visit their grandparents who lived up in the mountains in Southern California. One day, my dad was outside playing and he ran back to the house excited, telling my grandparents that he found baby lizards that were sticking their tongues out at him. My great-grandpa asked to see the lizards, so my dad took him to the spot. Turns out, my dad wasn't playing with lizards, but with baby rattle snakes. He had stumbled upon their nest. It's weird to think about, but if something went wrong in that situation he would have been toast…. and I wouldn't be here.

The same thing could be said of my grandpa who fought in WWII. If he didn't make it out, our family tree would have looked sensationally different. That kind of thing goes on and on. Our families have stories and events that could have gone one way or the other. It's weird to think about how tiny moments going the right way are the reasons we're here.

When we begin to look at our lives through the lens of a rich back-story, full of providence, everything doesn't seem quite so random. Perhaps we should give credit to the choices made that have brought us to where we are today. Our future is largely connected with our past. We don't have to repeat where we've been, but without the past, we wouldn't be where we are today.

With all that being said, we should remember that today is an important moment too. We are standing at the precipice of the rest of our lives. Where we go from here and what we do from this point forward has ramifications for our future. Most of us don't like to consider that what we do today is going to be felt two, three, or even five years from now. That seems like too much responsibility. But this is part of getting older and wiser, and learning to count our days, because we never know when our number will be called. This present moment is a gift; an adventure to be lived. No one is going to live it for us. It's up to us.

God has set a fire in our hearts for this kind of life. There is a longing inside us to be wanderers. To go from here to there—living, breathing, challenging, and gaining understanding. There is something so freeing, so beautiful about adventure.

Being out on the road has always been an incredible experience for me. I love long drives. There is something so liberating about being on the open road that lights a fire in our hearts. In his best selling book, *On the Road,*[7] Jack Keruoak tells a story about a series of epic road trips. He talks about heading west and shares about what happens along the way of traveling. The miles have a way of changing perspective; the distance influences us in a profound way. There is this description Jack shares about having no place to go but everywhere, and so we drive forward and let the stars be our guides.

When we rise up to meet the road before us, ever tackling it along the way, we continue to grow with God. And the whole time, God is smiling and directing and is excited to see where we go next. It's a beautiful picture of our heavenly Father who knows us and loves us and is waiting for us. It makes us think a lot about this life that God has given. Who do we want to be? Where do we want to go?

God has allowed us to be made new through Him and in Him. He is creating you and me into His image. That is beautiful. That is true. Sometimes we miss that. Sometimes we forget this life is an adventure in finding our way onward. Sometimes we forget growing up is a tragically beautiful experience in finding God and ourselves. We are here on this earth, but there is more to the adventure than what we see and hear. This is just the beginning of a beautiful journey. Every great adventure starts with one small step and this is it—take that step. Our lives matter. Our lives echo eternity, calling forth a great, great adventure.

Our heavenly Father knows what greatness waits. If we take that step, we'll see how our adventure is really a journey onwards.

Growing up is all the rage because it is through growing up and getting older that we move onward in our lives. Getting older doesn't guarantee us getting closer to Jesus, but it can. We learn to navigate the changing waters around us and reconcile all things to God. This is the beautifully redemptive part of growing up. Some have mistaken growing up as getting closer to the end, but we know, as the years pile up, that we are only getting closer to life. We are beginning to see the beauty and sacredness of life in the here and now. We are beginning to see that we are caught *in between*.

Like a Journey

Following Jesus is not simply a one-time decision. It is the acceptance of a new journey.

There is this peculiar part in the gospel of Luke after Jesus has died on the cross.[8] Towards the end of the book, Jesus comes back to His followers, but they don't recognize Him. He is literally walking and talking with them, but they don't know it's Him. The text says they are walking "along the way" when Jesus meets them. They continue down this road and share a meal together. It's during the meal—when Jesus breaks the bread—that they recognize Him. Then, in great Houdini fashion, He disappears, and they realize what had just happened—they had been walking down the road with Jesus.

The gospel writer Luke was actually a clever novelist, a first century Ernest Hemingway of sorts. The gospels are typically categorized as "Historical Narrative." They tell the story of Jesus and are heavy on the philosophical and didactic side of things.

Sometimes we fail to see the narrative side of the gospels. Luke understood symbolism, foreshadowing, and character development. All one has to do is read about Peter from the beginning of The Gospel of Luke to the author's second book, Acts, to see his transformation. He changes quite a bit. So, when Luke mentions "along the way" he is alluding to something. It's not random happenstance that Jesus meets his followers while they are walking on the road; it's actually quite intentional.

The first followers of Jesus actually weren't called Christians. That term wasn't developed until a later time. At first, they were called followers of *The Way*. It's a Greek word (*hodos*) that also means *road* or *street*. The idea behind it was that these early followers of Jesus were a group of people who followed a certain road, a path of life. Someone in the first century saw their commitment to Jesus and came up with this nickname—they are following the way of Jesus, the One who went before them. It is His life that they are mimicking, trying to do things the way He did. So, towards the end of Luke, Jesus starts walking with His followers who are heading towards Jerusalem, the place He tells them to start from in His next book. Jesus' apparition is a reminder to keep walking, keep following the road ahead. He is encouraging His followers to continue the journey they began with Him.

Have you ever noticed how most great stories include a journey? It's an *Odyssey*.[9] It's about going *There and Back Again*;[10] or, it's leaving something familiar, like a cupboard under the stairs, and walking towards your destiny a la *Harry Potter*.[11] Often times, great stories have to do with leaving the current place and heading somewhere new.

Christianity is best understood as a journey. Following Jesus is like setting out for an epic excursion from here to there. We pack our bags for the road, our gaze transfixed on the horizon, and we head out towards the unknown. How many of us would be comfortable with such a trip? As His followers, we have a road to walk down; a road that is rugged and vertiginous. We may experience hardship and spiritual vertigo; we may falter and fall from the path, but we may also receive so much more than we give.

In life there come points, tipping points really, where we are compelled to do something regardless of what other people may think. The entire world could be against us, but that doesn't matter when we're convicted in our own hearts. We feel as if whatever it is that stands before us can and will be overcome. I imagine we've all felt that way before.

It's when our faith intersects with our daily lives that we have a decision to make. We can either continue to live how we are now, not changing anything, sort of staying in a perpetual circle of ordinary, or we can choose to break out of the mold and out of the routine. God places something on our heart that is bold, revolutionary, and well, difficult. It's a make or break moment, and we can make the choice to go for it. We can take the risk to jump before looking.

You've probably discovered that following Jesus down this road isn't what you expected it to be at the start. Perhaps you've been going down this path for a while—listening to sermons, attending church, reading good books—and your path has always gone one way, but now you're challenged to walk another. The truth is, you can spend your whole life living in the past, or prepare for the bright future ahead of you.

I knew a girl who worked at a coffee shop around the corner from our church. During my weekly coffee trips I got to know her and found out she had recently moved to California because she was starting over. She started coming to our church and we'd talk about what it meant to "start over." Now, whenever people say they're starting over, I get excited, because I know that means they are ready for a change. It means… they're ready to try a different path.

Their life led them in one direction, but now they want to start a different journey. People with that resolve are ones who are preparing to meet Jesus. Sometimes moving and leaving are actually connected to spirituality. As my friend from the coffee shop discovered, the act of moving led her to encounter Jesus.

God has laid a path before us and invites us to become followers of a different way, His way. The road is long and winding, but followers of Jesus embrace it, even in uncertainty, with passion and love because that is the only way to keep going. It's like the poet, Robert Frost, once said: "Two roads diverged in the woods and I, I took the one less traveled by, and that has made all the difference."[12]

The longest journey begins with a single step.

I've had a few people tell me over the years that I was an "introspective" person—always taking the time to look inside and think over what was going on in my life. I suppose I've been that way for years.

Growing up in the church, I remember going through that thinking process even from a young age. If you grew up in the church, then you understand this weird dynamic that happens twice a year known as the "Church Musical." For some reason this was a big fad back in the eighties and nineties in the church—low budget musicals starring kids, sans any real musical talent.

So I was in the Christmas musical a few times growing up. I had differing roles, usually as a background character where my lines and stage time were limited. I never got the spotlight. I remember that my little brother was cast as baby Jesus once, which wasn't really fair, I thought, since he was just born a few months before. I thought that role kind of fell in his lap. He didn't have any lines either. He just lay there and cried.

Anyway, my best role over the years of tumultuous musicals was the ubiquitous shepherd in the Christmas musical. Seriously, all I did was walk down the aisle, carrying my shepherd's staff and stand on the stage during a rendition of "Glory in Eclesio Deo" along with like twenty other shepherds. I remember there was this girl in my grade who got cast as an angel. In the dress rehearsal room, she looked at me and said something to the effect of, "Oh you're only a shepherd. Ha. I'm an angel…and you suck."

Now I don't know if she said that last part, but I remember the feeling of "not good enough" even in the Christmas musical. There was a hierarchy in the nativity scene. The angels and wise men had a superiority complex. If you didn't think there was a class dynamic happening in church musicals, I'm here to tell you that there was. Alas, it was the story of my childhood: Always the shepherd, never the angel.

That was just another opportunity for me to be introspective and wonder *Why me? Why this? Why now?* I think most of us, if we're honest, ask those questions all the time. They are questions of hope, but also desperation. We want to know the "why" behind events and relationships in our lives. The problem, however, is we don't always find those answers easily. If this life is like a journey, then it is a winding path of lots of questions and not many answers.

We love movies and stories, in part, because they have closure. Things work out, and after two hours, a resolution comes across the screen. But life isn't like that—the resolution doesn't always come when we want it, so we just struggle to make sense of things that aren't evolving and aren't concluding. Ten years ago, I thought about some of the same things I'm still thinking of now. I'm looking down the tracks of life and seeing that it's still just as confusing and complicated as it was then. Not much has changed in that sense, and I don't think it ever will. Time doesn't always grant answers, but it does grant perspective.

I have a number of family members who are family not by blood but by choice—which are the best kind after all. One of my favorite people in the entire world is someone I called my Uncle Martin. He was the father of one of my mom's best friends, and he was always simply known as Uncle Martin to me. He became sort of a pseudo-grandpa for me over the years and has impacted my life in ways I can't even begin to describe. I used to ride on his shoulders at the San Diego Zoo. I used to sit next to him at SeaWorld, holding a churro in one hand and his hand in the other. My childhood is full of memories that came from him and our time together. He taught me about life in ways that I'm sure he wasn't even aware of at the time.

One of our favorite spots to explore was Old Town San Diego. My Uncle Martin and I used to go here when I was younger, walking the dirt roads, looking inside the old gift shops, and munching on chips and salsa. One trip a couple years ago felt different. I finally realized that my uncle had slowed down. He wasn't able to walk like he used to. So, instead of walking around the block, we found a spot on a bench and just soaked in the warm sun. I sat there next to someone who had been there for me growing up, and we spoke about life.

He told me that he was just waiting to die. When someone says something like that, we usually react quite dramatically. We say things like, "No! Don't say that! You have so much to live for." And we go on and on with our reasons, bemoaning the fact that someone would even, just for a second, contemplate death. Truth be told, his words freaked me out a bit. But I soon learned that for my Uncle Martin, preparing to die wasn't an escape from this life. It was the words of someone who had done his journey in this life and was ready for the next part.

On that bench with my Uncle Martin, I began to realize what he meant by being ready to die. It wasn't a morbid request, but a genuine, honest statement about preparing for what he knew was inevitable.

I see a lot of people who are trying so hard to guard their life, to protect it instead of surrendering it. No one wants to face the truth that one day the tracks of this life run out. One day the journey will end. My Uncle Martin understood this.

I guess I'm learning that life in many ways means confusion and tension because there are many things that don't resolve and never will. Nevertheless, we march forward. We continue this journey, uncertain of what it holds, but unbelievably confident of the One we're following after.

I've always found that story of Jesus on the road to Emmaus kind of peculiar. Jesus asks questions that He already knows the answers to and doesn't reveal who He is until the last moment. I kind of wondered if that was Jesus just messing with His followers. ("But I am Jesus!" and the crowd starts oohing and ahhing like a rap battle.) But there is a deeper message in this story.

The text says their "hearts were burning along the road" while He spoke to them. They knew something was at work. If they were only willing to open their eyes, they would have seen the truth.

Jesus still meets us along the road. He still meets us on the journey, directing our paths to Him. He isn't shouting directions from Heaven saying, "Go this way or that way," but He meets us where we are and walks this journey with us. And our hearts catch fire in the same way.

If I could travel back in time and meet my eighteen year old self, someone who was green, full of hope, and completely naïve, I'd say a simple thing—"Keep walking forward." This is what we all need to do. Cherish the journey and keep moving forward, winding down the path set before us. We have a God who is leading us from Earth to Eternity. We may be at different points in this journey so far, but it is God who is with us, guiding us forward.

I'm learning this life is really best understood as an epic voyage. Our backstory may be rich and varied, with ups and downs marking the winding path we've wandered to get to this point. We must live with all those complexities. We must live with faith and doubt. God is big enough to handle both. He calls us forward, one step at a time. If this life is truly a journey, then boldly we put one foot in front of the other, and march on until Heaven meets Earth. We embrace being *caught in between.*

Memorable Moments

I'm learning life often has a lot to teach us when we take a deeper look. There is more happening around us and in us then we often realize.

I've had these moments throughout my life where I realized there was more going on than what appeared on the surface.

Oftentimes, we talk about embracing the grandness of the moment, but what about when the moment grabs ahold of us? At the end of the movie *Boyhood* this sentiment is shared as the main character reflects on life and what it means to be aware of what is happening around him. He says, "You know how everyone's always saying, "Seize the moment"? I don't know, I'm kind of thinking it's the other way around, you know, like the moment seizes us."[13] I love that.

A couple of years ago I went to a Damien Rice concert at the Greek Theatre in Los Angeles. The Greek is an amphitheater entirely outdoors, with rows of seats slanted up on a hill. The stage faces up this hill, so the entire venue has incredible acoustics. During the show, Damien Rice sang his Irish melancholy heart out. I'm part Irish so I understand the despondent lyrics and general moody feeling of most of his songs. It speaks to me, reminding me that sometimes things aren't right in the world and I deal with it.

At one point in the show, Damien played one of my favorite songs of his, *Cannonball*.[14] I remember the whole thing vividly, like it just happened. He played the song passionately, strumming his capo-clad guitar, singing his soul out, hitting notes in the upper register of his voice that would make Whitney Houston do a double take. Then, in a moment of brash spontaneity, he ripped his auxiliary chord out of his guitar and kicked over his microphone.

After a loud snap, crackle and pop sound, like he'd poured the world's largest bowl of Rice Krispies, he continued to play. It was nothing but his voice and an unplugged acoustic guitar. The strange thing about it was I could hear him perfectly. No one sang along. No one laughed or clapped. It was utterly and eerily silent. The music spoke for itself. The vulnerability of that moment is etched in my memory and is something I won't soon forget. I will always remember when Damien Rice literally went unplugged in concert and the Greek Theatre was silent.

After a while, we begin to see how many of these significant moments exist in our lives. Years add on, and we witness the growing stockpile of memories and experiences that matter. In the world of screenplays and writing, we call these major moments "story turns."

Donald Miller wrote about this in his book *A Million Miles in A Thousand Years.*[15] A "story turn" is when a character walks through a door that he can't walk back out of. The experience, or the scene, leaves an indelible mark on who he is and who he is becoming. It's defining and definitive. By default, life has its own set of story turns we're experiencing. By the time someone turns thirty, they've had around fifteen major story turns that are both positive and negative in nature, moments that have changed them one way or the other. In time, these story turns become major focal points of their personal narrative. That is to say, they are written on the pages of their life to be remembered by you and others.

I can recall several of my major *story turn* moments. These are moments that stick out to me that have been full of love and pain, courage and fear. These moments have made me who I am today. A powerful exercise is to take an inventory of our lives life and the experiences we've shared, and consider what the overall theme would be? That is a question I asked myself. Would someone be able to read or see these scenes and know the type of man I am? What is the legacy I'd want others to see?

There is this scene in the Book of Joshua that reminds me a bit about significant *story turns.* After the Israelites are delivered from the hands of the Egyptians, and after they have wandered the desert for forty years, they finally make it to the Promised Land. At this point, Moses is gone and a new leader has emerged. His name is Joshua. His predecessor was a great leader and followed God faithfully, but we learn that God isn't interested in another Moses— now He wants a Joshua.

In the third chapter of the Book of Joshua, we learn that Joshua and the people approach the Jordan River.[16] In order to attain the Promised Land, they must first cross this body of water. This is significant for a few reasons. First, any time people cross water in the Bible something important is happening. Crossing water signified movement and often God's provision. Secondly, Moses was the leader to take the people through the Red Sea; now, Joshua has the opportunity to lead the people through water as well. His leadership is being solidified in the eyes of the people. In the story, God enables the people to walk through the water onto dry ground, just like they did in Egypt.

He leads them forward, to a place they've never been before. And God gives this compelling message to the people: "Follow me because this is a way you've never been before." Essentially, God is saying, "We are doing something new, going to a place you are unfamiliar with, so let me lead you." God is setting the people up for a truly significant moment. In terms of the character development of Israel, this is a scene that is going to stick.

Finally, after everyone has crossed over the Jordan River, God invites the people to cement this event in their memory banks. He invites them to remember this *story turn*. God orders Joshua to have an altar built on the side of the river. The priests of the people are directed to gather twelve stones and arrange them on the side, which will prove to be a vivid testament to what had happened that day.

God says that this altar or memorial will be a sign to future generations. When they come to the river, they will see this altar, this sign, and ask, "What do these stones mean?" Then, at that moment, there is an opportunity to share how God dried up the Jordan River to lead His people across to the Promised Land. This altar of stones is not for God; rather, it is a visual reminder to His people that something significant happened there. It is a permanent sign that lives were forever altered from this point forward. It makes us think: What kind of moments are we being remembered for?

It's an interesting exercise, but if we imagined our lives like a movie, would people know the plot? Would they understand what the character is striving for?

My wife and I traveled to the Hawaiian island of Oahu a couple years back. After days of exploring the island, drinking fruity concoctions, and bathing in the warm Pacific, we decided to do a little sight seeing. On the top of my list was to visit Pearl Harbor.

Pearl Harbor is probably one of the more emotionally moving places I've ever been. I remember driving up to the spot.

Our car reached the top of a hill, and all of a sudden, the harbor emerged in a panoramic view. We stared into it as we drove down the slope and eventually parked our car. From the very moment we set foot on this place, the feeling of significance took a hold of us.

We walked around the harbor and it honestly felt like hallowed ground. We got on a boat and went out in the water. I found myself staring up into the sky and surrounding shores, trying to envision what it might have looked like that day so many years ago with both sides of the fighting overwhelmed with nerves and despair, knowing how final this attack was.

There is still a ship buried at the bottom of the sea. Our tour boat gently glided over this water grave where young men with very old bones still reside. No one talked or took pictures here. In fact, it was remarkably quiet. Everyone who comes here understands the sheer significance of this place.

As we traveled back to shore, I witnessed a beautiful gesture. A group of Japanese tourists knelt down by the waters edge and placed a few flowers in the harbor. One lady knelt down and touched the water as she laid flower atop it.

No one goes to Pearl Harbor without understanding the loss, pain and incredible bravery experienced at this place. No one goes here without asking the question, "What does this place mean?" And no one leaves without someone explaining the significance of what happened there.

Most of us do this with the moments in our lives. We snap photos and take souvenirs. We hang up degrees and awards, displaying our achievements and accolades. In many ways, we make our own mini altars to remember what happened.

The day Israel crossed the Jordan River, God was giving them a reminder that this would be a day they would never forget. People would look upon it and remember in detail what transpired years earlier.

It makes us think: Is there something about our lives that entreats others to ask a question about why we are the way we are? Do people look at us and ask, "What happened there?" I guess this is to say, is their something different about the way we live? Is it a collection of memorable scenes, of significant moments that have made us into the people we are today? Furthermore, do we have the courage to take hold of life and make these scenes happen?

One September, I was asked to be a speaker for a family camp in northern California. The camp was to be held right outside of Yosemite. It was a beautiful place. The camp was full of wild life, ginormous trees, and a beautiful, pristine lake. One afternoon towards the end of the camp, my wife and I were hanging out in the lake on paddle boats. On the other side of the lake was a large flume slide. I had never seen anything like it before in my life.

The slide was several feet tall and declined at a sharp angle from the top until the very bottom where it pointed up towards the sky. Someone would slide down and then when they reached the bottom, they would be shot up into the sky and descend until they crashed into the water below. It was very dangerous and also quite compelling.

I sat there watching person after person fly down this slide at unflagging speed only to be launched effortlessly into the air and land in the water below. It looked painful and fun, and something that insurance companies would call a nightmare. I was sitting in our paddleboat in jeans, enjoying the afternoon, when someone called from the side of the lake, entreating me to go down the flume slide.

I remember yelling, "I'm wearing jeans." Incidentally, this is kind of a weird thing to yell out if no one around you knows the context of the situation. The response I received back was something to the effect of, "So…?"

With a little prodding from my wife, we paddled over towards the side of the lake. I emptied my pockets of my phone and wallet and grabbed a foam mat for the slide. I hiked up the steep incline were the flume slide rested and prepared to let myself go. I distinctly remember the feeling once I started down the slide. It was the kind where your stomach rises to your throat and back again several times. My foam mat was airborne and I soared into the air right before gravity took its effect and I slammed down into the water below. Several cheers emanated from the sidelines as I swam towards the shore. Soaking wet, with a huge smile on my face, I ran up the incline again, ready to try the slide a second time.

The result was tantamount to the first time; I went down—velocity plus flight and a landing into the water below. As I stood on the shore of the lake, I realized something about life. It's seems rather obvious, but life is full of opportunities to make the most of what is before you. There are umpteen, often unforeseen, events that can transpire if we have the courage and hope to pursue them. Whether it is tackling a flume slide at a family camp or taking a bold move to pursue a new career, love interest, or hobby, the opportunities are before us.

I wonder if the Israelites saw the Jordan River as a memory to be made. I wonder if they were able to look past the obstacle that laid before them and think about what would happen on the other side—to realize that after this event there would be stories to tell. John Lennon is quoted as saying, "Life is what happens while we're making other plans."[17] I think John has it right. We can get lost in life, sort of meander through it with big hopes and dreams, not realizing that every moment is a chance to live and thrive.

Life is full of meaningful opportunities to relish in grace and truth. Are we gathering memories to tell the world? Are we giving them an opportunity to see us and ask, "What happened there?"

The same themes that give us compelling stories on the screen are the ones that give us compelling stories in life. Do we understand the beauty of living to the full? Do we seek to make memorable moments in our lives?

I was in Chile working with a church for a couple weeks when I learned something beautiful about Chilean culture. People love to be together and party. I was at a barbecue on a Sunday after church. We gathered outside and ate and drank and laughed together. After the meal, one of my friends got out a guitar and started strumming chords. With glasses of wine filled to the brim, we toasted one another and sang revolution songs.

There's a saying in Chile, that there is always something to celebrate…even the dog's birthday. I love that perspective. Life is grand and good and beautiful. There is always reason to capture the moment. There is always reason to make a memorable scene. Making memorable moments is learning to see the sacredness of what's happening now. It's about existing *in between.*

Memorable moments are created when we grab life with both hands and share it with one another. It's when we embrace the beauty of the here and now, aware that more is happening around us and in us than just "what we see" or "what appears on" the surface.

Beautiful moments surround us everyday. Seize them. And let's not be afraid to the let the moment seize us every once in a while. Who knows? We might look back one day and say, "What happened there?" "What happened," we'll reply, "is that we were aware of being *caught in between.*"

Ordinary Wonder

God has given us this life as a wonderful adventure. It's our task to open our eyes to the beauty and wonder that surrounds us.

I have a friend named Paul who is an incredible surfer. He's been surfing for most of his life and riding waves for him is as natural as breathing. Recently, Paul and I drove to a local surf spot in California called Bolsa Chica. We got up early, before the sun poked its head above the clouds, and drove to the beach. We zipped up our wetsuits and made the journey from dry to wet sand, getting in the water and paddling out. The sea was raging this particular morning. It was choppy and paddling out was a challenge in and of itself. I struggled all morning to catch a wave. Either I wasn't fast enough or couldn't find my footing. I fell quickly and often, spending most of my time watching waves crash on the shore. Paul didn't have much luck either.

We took a small break and sat on our boards to watch the horizon. We bobbed up and down as the swells passed under us, our gaze fixated on the beautiful open ocean. Suddenly, we had a moment in the ocean that no surfer wants to encounter. Grey fins surrounded us. They ominously protruded out of the water and made their way towards our boards. If you've ever been in the ocean and you see a fin, your heart stops. The likelihood of it being a shark is slim, but your heart skips a beat nonetheless. Our fears were soon alleviated, though, when we saw dolphins passing through. We reached out our hands and let the pod of dolphins graze past. I realized I could pay to go to Seaworld and touch a dolphin, or I could just sit in the ocean, and they would come to me.

In that moment I thought about all the other things I could be doing, and yet here I was sitting on a surfboard watching dolphins swim past. My heart was full, and I had this familiar ache of joy. The reaction I was experiencing was wonder.

When was the last time you allowed yourself to be lost in the wonder of your existence?

I often question if what our churches are lacking is not greater theological or ministerial training, but a lack of wonder seeping into our lives. Wonder allows us to see God for who He is and be overwhelmed in the process. Wonder unveils covered eyes to the goodness, and radical creative energy of God.

One of the highlights of any church calendar is summer and winter camps. We uproot ourselves from familiar surroundings and place ourselves in environments where we can see and hear more clearly. By getting out of what is familiar, and going into nature, we provide ourselves with an opportunity for wonder. Living in Southern California, we have two seasons: summer and not summer. Summer is what happens when the temperature soars, and the days are long and the nights warm. Summer is beautiful. "Not summer" happens for the rest of the year—there is still sun, but it's a little cooler. Needless to say, we don't get snow very often.

One year for winter camp, we drove to the mountains. The news forecasted a huge snowstorm for the weekend, so everyone was excited to see what that might mean. The kids' faces were struck with awe as we traveled in our bus to camp, watching the snow falling all around us. Once we arrived and unloaded our vans, we made our way to the first session. I saw students engaging with one another and God. They sang their hearts out, laughed, and connected with each other. But later that night is when I saw them capture wonder.

After the session ended, we made our way back to the cabins. The sky opened up, and snow began to fall like Heaven just opened up a million bags of cotton balls. All of a sudden, students left the comfort of the cabin to dance in the snow. Some of them made snow angels and threw snowballs at one another; others simply stood still with their heads tilted back. We took our freshman students and buried them in the snow. And they loved every second of it. We played and laughed and broke the quiet time curfew, but it didn't matter.

When we returned from camp, I asked our students to tell me their favorite part of the weekend. No one said the speaker or the worship or the big group games. I was disappointed at first. The students assured me they loved the sessions and small groups, but what spoke most to their hearts was the night in the snow. And then I realized something: God was present in the speaker and the time of worship, but He was also present in the snow.

Our hearts are designed for wonder. God wired us to be people who live everyday with wondrous curiosity because God is intrinsically linked to creation. We see Him in beauty and art; we feel Him in the hustle and bustle of life. Our God is present. He is in the wind, the music, and the laughter. He is in the snow. And sometimes we miss this.

In the movie *The Great Dictator*,[18] Charlie Chaplin delivers a powerful performance as both an actor and director. Chaplin creates a whimsical tale of Hitler and his doppelganger, who, ironically, is a Jewish barber. Towards the end of the movie, Chaplin has pulled off a *Prince and the Pauper* switch between the two. The Jewish barber is mistaken for the Hitler character and is given an opportunity to give a speech with the world listening in. What happens next might be some of the greatest writing to ever grace the silver screen. My favorite line from the film is what Chaplin says in an epic final speech, that people "have the power to make this life free and beautiful, to make this life a wonderful adventure."

How often do we forget this life is a beautiful, epic, serendipitous journey that came forth from God's stunning creativity? He created such variety: mountains, oceans, trees, streams, rocks, fields, deserts, and chocolate. How often do we miss the everyday wonder of life?

There is a peculiar teaching in the Scriptures where Jesus talks about old and new wine skins. A wine skin was a pouch of sorts, constructed to hold the liquid intact. He uses this metaphor as an example of what happens when we force the old into the new. The context of Jesus' wineskin discussions was how someone would need to approach Jesus with new faith that couldn't fit with the faith of old.

I wonder if we treat our lives like the wineskins. Instead of rising every day as if it were new, we try and live today like it's yesterday; we try and force the past into the present.

I've heard it said that one of the greatest tricks of the enemy is causing us to forget. We forget where we've been. We forget where we've come from and what we've overcome. Remembering is powerful. It reveals to us how we've survived trials and tests that have come our way. An active memory shows us we've been through darkness and found the light peeking in through the cracks. We've fallen down, but now we are able to arise. How often do we forget the wonders we've experienced?

The Scriptures say the One in us is greater than the one in the world (1 John 4:4). That's a promise we can't forget. We must fight to remember it. We must fight to see the wonder that is here in us and around us. If life is meant to be a dance with God, we need to hear the music.

We have a choice to join this dance. We have a choice to see wonder. What if we began to develop a rhythm of wonder in our lives? Rather than meander aimlessly through the day, what if we intentionally took time to rest in His wonder? Would that be enough for us? Can we begin to live in the continual wonder of God?

I had a friend in college who was one of those philosophical types. You know the ones. They spend a great deal of their time sitting around drinking coffee and staring off into space. A productive day for them is one in which they wrapped their mind around an idea for a couple of hours, think about it, and then don't reach any conclusion at all. My friend used to do that on most days. One time I came by his room to watch a movie, and he was sitting on his bed, staring off into space. I knew he was caught in one of his think tank modes, so I approached cautiously.

He turned to me and asked a simple, but haunting question. "How do you think God feels when we say we're bored?"

It was a good question. I realized he'd probably spent the better part of his day thinking it through and probably didn't have a firm grasp on the answer, but he had thought about it to death. I leaned up against his dresser and stared off into space with him, watching the question dance around the room. It made me think.

I wondered if God is disappointed or frustrated by the word "bored." Usually we say we're bored when things feel monotonous or mundane. My friend said he had thought about that, too. But then he told me about a theologian named G.K. Chesteron who wrote about monotony in nature.[19] Chesteron argued that the sun rising everyday or daisies blooming in the spring were not mundane activities for God. What if, instead, God awakened the world each day with the sun rising and the flowers blooming using the same intensity and excitement as when He originally created life? What if every day was exciting and new for God?

I had never thought about it like that before. G.K. Chesteron wondered if God had an eternal appetite of infancy. Repetition in the universe was not a predictable recurrence, but a theatrical encore. Maybe God never gets tired of calling forth the sun and moon, and making each flower beautiful. Maybe God never grows restless in reveling in the beauty of the created realm. If it's true, perhaps, then, God doesn't know the feeling of boredom. It's something we've created. And maybe we've created it because we've forgotten the wonder of life.

My friend told me that he never says he's bored anymore. He's deleted the word from his vocabulary because it's an insult to God. He said that we've often taught in the church that taking the Lord's name in vain is sin. But shouldn't it be a sin, too, when we take His glory in vain? Doesn't it grieve God's heart the same when we take this gift of life and let it pass us by without actually living it?

The pulse of Heaven pumps our hearts everyday. It is a choice, though, to live in the infinite wonder of the God Who creates and recreates. This is the God Who doesn't get bored and Who has given us a life where everything is new. He calls forth the sun to beckon a new adventure and brings out the moon as a grand finale. I've started to seek wonder because I know it exists. It's ordinary in a sense that it happens everyday. But just because something happens everyday doesn't mean it's ordinary.

I love the ending scene of the movie *The Graduate*.[20] The main character, Ben, has been involved with an older woman named Mrs. Robinson who seduces him into an illicit affair. Eventually, though, he pulls away from that relationship when he falls in love with her daughter, Elaine. After discovering he used to be involved with her mother, Elaine leaves Ben. She goes to pursue another life and is to be married.

Towards the end of the movie, Ben is driving, trying to find

Elaine. He arrives at the church where she is marrying someone else. He stands above the sanctuary in the balcony. A sheet of glass separates him from those down below. He begins to pound on the glass and yell out her name. Elaine glances up and sees him. She begins to walk down the aisle.

People are telling her what to do, but we can't hear them; we only see their mouths moving. Finally, she yells out to Ben, and he runs down to her. After shaking off her father who meets him at the stairs, he pushes the crowd back. He then grabs a giant cross and fights off the crowd of people, swinging it in front of them. Ben and Elaine then run out the front door and jam the cross into the outside doors so no one can get out. Hand-in-hand they run toward the street and board a bus. The song *Sound of Silence* by Simon and Garfunkel begins to play as they drive off.

Elaine goes after "the adventure," not the predictable life that was planned for her. She uncovers in the film that this life is full of beauty and wonder, and she can live life the way she wants.

A while back, a girl who graduated from our church youth group came back one night. She showed up out of nowhere, which she usually does when life throws something unpredictable her way. We sat in the sanctuary, and she wondered where her life was going. She was trying to decide between staying in school or moving in with a boyfriend. I remember how scared she was and also how defeated she was. Over and over again, she told me, "I don't want my life to turn out this way. I don't want to be pregnant, with a bunch of kids, and for them to have a deadbeat dad. I don't want to be stuck in a job and hate my life."

I listened to her share her concerns and worries, and something struck me. She never once talked about what she *actually* wanted. Everything she said was negative and reactive. So, in a moment of brash confidence, I decided to say what was on my heart without fear of how it might come off. I told her that she didn't have to go down that path, but the choice to be different started today. The adventure was hers to create. She left that night with a confidence I hadn't seen in her before. She didn't know how things would turn out, but knew the choice was up to her.

Paul writes in 1 Corinthians 6:2 that "today is the day of Salvation." Now is the time to change, for who knows what tomorrow will bring?

This life is a wonderful adventure. When we open our eyes to see life for what it is, we gain clarity for how we live. The more I try and live this way, the more I'm beginning to learn there are no ordinary days. There's just wonder that repeats day-by-day and week-by-week.

Let's open our eyes to see the adventure in front of us. Perhaps we'll be amazed at what happens when we pay attention to the wonder that surrounds us—the wonder of being *caught in between.*

ACT II: Seeing Beyond

"Life is either a daring adventure or nothing at all." Helen Keller[21]

"In this world you will have trouble, but take heart; I have overcome the world." John 16:33 NIV

Being Caught in between is about seeing the glimpses of Heaven that come our way. It's about seeing more than what is here, realizing God often reveals Himself to us and speaks to us through everyday activities. The people we meet, the books we read, and the movies we see are all part of this grand adventure of learning to *see beyond*.

God Likes to Party

What if signs of the Kingdom are closer than we realize? What if there are ordinary life occurrences full of deeper meaning? Have you ever been to a party or gathering of family and friends that seemed to never end? If you have, perhaps you've tasted a bit of Heaven in the here and now.

Jesus was asked the question, "What is the greatest commandment?" a few times in the gospels.[22] It was honestly a good question. The audience was essentially saying, "What is the way to exist fully and truly?" In the different contexts of the Gospels we see how this question wasn't always asked genuinely, but used to trap or trick Jesus. In typical disarming fashion, He responds brilliantly. He recites one of the most important Jewish prayers, the Shema. The Shema comes from the Old Testament, in the book of Deuteronomy.[23] It was a prayer said multiple times a day by all members of Jewish society. Jesus recites this prayer that says to "love the Lord your God with all your heart, soul, mind and strength" and people probably nodded in approval.

Everyone knew the Shema was the number one commandment, but what about the second? There was some debate here. The great keepers of Jewish thought and tradition, rabbis, disagreed on what the second greatest commandment was.

We know historically there was a strong movement to study under rabbis during the time of Jesus. Students would follow their rabbis around, learning about life and God from these sought after sages of the Jewish faith. They would follow their rabbis down the street when they were shopping; they would hang out with them at the market, or the café; some texts even suggest disciples would follow their Rabbis into the bathroom, just to see if they said anything life changing. There is even an account of a student following his rabbi into his house at night and sleeping underneath his bed (not sure how the Rabbi's wife felt about this). Jesus was a rabbi, too, and had followers, which included the twelve apostles and others.

However, before Jesus came on the scene, there were two very famous rabbis that people followed, and these rabbinical minds actually had founded two distinct schools of thought. Their names were Rabbi Shammai and Rabbi Hillel.[24] These rabbis had similarities and differences, areas of theology where they agreed and others where they were opposed. For example, both Shammai and Hillel agreed that the greatest commandment was the Shema—Love the Lord Your God with heart, mind, soul, and strength. But they differed on what was the second. Shammai taught the second greatest commandment was to "Be holy as the Lord is holy." A lot of Jewish people followed this teaching. They made sure personal holiness was at the top of their to-do list. They avoided eating certain foods and touching unclean people and places, and they focused keeping themselves separate from things that could compromise their holiness.

Hillel, on the other hand, taught that the second greatest commandment was to love your neighbor as yourself. These two rabbis differed on the second greatest commandment, and like any good differentiation between various parties, numerous debates ensued. Interestingly, Jesus sides with Hillel. The second greatest commandment, according to Jesus, is to love your neighbor as yourself.

The more we read the Scriptures and look at the life of Christ, we see how love is the essence of Christian faith. It always has been and always will be.

In Luke's version of the famous question, (Luke 10) an expert of the law confronts Jesus and asks Him to share His opinion. Jesus answers with the Shema, but then follows up his answer with a famous story called the Parable of the Good Samaritan. It's one of those stories we've all heard a time or two, but when we really break down the meaning of the story, it's life changing. Luke talks about a man walking down a dangerous path from Jerusalem to Jericho. The path was well known for it's downward slope, as well as the many robbers who hide among caves, awaiting a wearisome traveler. A man happened to walk down this path and meet up with a few thugs from antiquity.

They rob him and beat him to a pulp, and he's left to die on the side of the road. It begins as a story with a need for a hero. But what follows is an interesting set of characters that appear to be the perfect heroes, saviors who can step in and right the wrong. Two very holy men have the chance to help this man, but they choose not to. One is a priest, and the other is a Levite. Both are holy men, with special positions of service to God, and both choose to walk around the man rather than help him. Many commentators believe this ancient road to Jericho was not very wide, so literally, they had to "step over" this man lying on the ground.

It begs the question, though—how easy is it to walk past someone?

We probably do it every day. We walk past the homeless and the suffering in our cities. And we also walk past hurt and pain; we rush through a conversation because something else has more importance to us. We walk over people in our lives that need our help. The priest and Levite walk past this man. They walk past a fellow brother, a fellow Jew.

The next part of the story is where Jesus, in His brilliance, tries to illicit a reaction. The third character, and the hero of the story, is not a man of special service to God, nor is he even a Jew. He is a Samaritan. This title may mean little to us now, but in ancient Jerusalem, a Samaritan was one of the more reprobate characters one could find. They were looked down upon with great disgust and disrespect. A Samaritan was a "half-breed" after all, someone who was only a half Jew, a reminder of their ugly past. They were not the folks a good Jewish person would have over for dinner. In fact, most Jews would go out of their way to travel around the region of Samaria to avoid making contact with anyone from there. There is a lot of tension, distrust, and vengeful feelings existing between the two people groups. All of this makes the story more meaningful because the hero is this hated person. You can imagine the reaction of this expert of the law when Jesus includes the Samaritan in the story.

The Samaritan not only cares for the wounded traveler and bandages his wounds, but also he forks over the money to provide him with extended care. The text tells us he pays enough money for this man to stay at the inn for two months and then he even tells the innkeeper he will pay more if needed. He saves this stranger's life and is also willing to keep providing resources to help him.

Jesus then ends this story by asking which man was truly a "neighbor." The expert in the law responds interestingly, saying, "The one who had mercy on him." He doesn't even call him a Samaritan; just the "one." We can imagine him even gritting his teeth with that answer. Jesus tells him to go and do likewise.

It's a story we've heard countless times, but why did Jesus tell it? Was He simply trying to teach a lesson about doing unto others, as you would have them to unto you? Was He talking about the importance of love? It seems like both of these themes are readily present in the story, but He is going somewhere else too. Jesus is revealing a problem with the human heart. He is unmasking the brokenness of hate, self-righteousness, and promoting racial equality. He is imploring the reader to change.

The more time I spend with Jesus, the more I am aware of the chasm that exists in my own heart. I've discovered a deep divide between who God desires me to be and who I really am. We've all been there, right? We proclaim we love others, and our actions may attest to this at times, but then there are the inconsistencies. At times, we withhold our love for our own self-righteous purposes. Instead of loving without conditions, we demand in our own subtle ways that people live like us, act like us, and even look like us before they can receive our acceptance.

I think we do this subconsciously, but there is a value-system we use to determine how much love we will show to someone. That's why the priest and the Levite in the story probably felt justified in their walking around the beaten man. To them, he was just a stranger, so why bother? I've experienced extreme amounts of love in this life. I've seen love that is only possible because a stronger force is at work. But I've also seen a kind of love that is biased and heartless.

There was this girl who came to church over the years named Caitlyn. She was a sweet girl, who had a good heart—you can tell that about someone in their demeanor— and she cared about people and truly wanted to embrace a better life. The problem, though, was she came from a troubled past. Her dad had split, leaving her and her sisters to survive life with her mom. She was constantly fighting with her mom, unable to have peace at home. Caitlyn would show up at church every week with another issue. And to complicate matters, there were the boy issues. She bounced around from guy to guy, always searching for safety and love, but never finding it. You know the story, right? We've all heard it, and we've all known people in this predicament. It breaks your heart.

We welcomed her to every event and service we ever had. She came to different outings and camps, and she made friends with people at church. And we prayed for her. She would get closer and further away at the same time. We were there when she got in trouble for underage drinking. We were counseling her when she was heart broken after another guy left. When her dad was involved in horrendous crime, she came running down my street, and we just held her and sat with her. I remember when she turned eighteen and got a fake ID and I told her how that was a bad idea.

And the thing about her story is that it's still a work in progress, like we all are. I'd be lying if I said she changed and turned her life around. As far as I know, she didn't. But loving others isn't about the result. It's not an achievement; it's a command of Jesus. We love without thinking about people as projects. We love because that is the only response that Jesus asks of us regardless of the situation.

When Jesus speaks about love, He isn't instructing us to put conditions on our love, like we have a quota to fill. We love others without question and unapologetically because we have been loved that way. The way of Jesus is a path marked by forgiveness, acceptance, and mercy.

When I think about God's attitude towards people and His outlook towards them, I can't help but think God likes to party. A good party is one where there is food and drink, friends and family, laughter and of course, dancing. All good parties have dancing. When you enter through the doors, you feel like you're home, like this party was planned especially for you. All of a sudden, our cares and worries go out the door, and all we have to do is dance. We realize that there is fun to be had by all.

Perhaps this is why we love birthday parties so much—they teach us something about God. A few summers ago, I experienced an "Ecuadorian" birthday party. It really is quite the affair. People gather for food, music, and fun. There is a cake that everyone eats, after you try and smash the birthday boy or girl's face in it, and there is a piñata. But this is no ordinary piñata. Rather than it hanging from a tree, with someone trying to smash it, the person having the birthday breaks the piñata open. It really is quite the scene. They stand on a chair and rip open the piñata, sending candy falling to the ground like shrapnel. Suddenly, everyone at the party rushes in and piles on top of the candy, grabbing piece after piece. It's a massive dog pile of fun. I asked someone why they do this and was told, "It's so everyone gets candy…because the party is for everyone."

God's family is sort of like this kind of birthday party. Invitations are sent out; the guests arrive, and everyone gets the prize. There are no qualifiers to come to the party. Some may stay for a long time; others may leave and return, and some never make it to the party. Nevertheless, we keep inviting them and enjoying their presence when they show up, which sometimes happens unexpectedly.

Parties reveal something deeper in our lives. They show us God and reveal a part of us made for living to the full. But the perfect party, the one that we can't help but see *beyond* when we attend, is a wedding.

I attended a wedding a few years ago that was probably my favorite wedding since my own. (We all are a little biased, aren't we?) The wedding was on a yacht on the Fourth of July. It doesn't get much cooler than that. This wedding was for our friends Wesley and Carly. They had a boat, fireworks, great food, and did I mention a boat? The couple wanted to enjoy their special day out at sea with family and friends, which in and of itself was a nice gesture. We set out that afternoon, floating on the sea with the sun shining down on the guests. The bride was radiant as she walked down the aisle. Everything was picturesque. You can imagine the sort of view you have on a yacht. The ocean surrounded us and engulfed us entirely. It felt like we were exploring the vast unknown oceans; we were sailors embarking on a new journey.

As the sun slowly set in the background, shades of orange and pink flooded the yacht, bouncing off the table's dinnerware. I remember thinking that night about dancing. We sat at our table and ate our food, but there was something calling us to get up and dance. So we did. We danced and celebrated together. Our dancing was given an enormous encore when fireworks erupted in the night sky overhead. It was one of those moments you never forget—a moment where you feel fully alive. Eventually, the yacht made its way back to the dock, but not without giving us memories of fun times on the open sea.

I attend a lot of weddings, some more fun than others, but each one has been a subtle reminder: there are things in life worth celebrating. Regardless of family backgrounds or cultures, people celebrate momentous occasions. We may celebrate love, like weddings; achievements, like graduations and promotions; life, like the birth of a child or a birthday; and special holidays that mean something to our family and friends. If you really think about it, several times a year we carve out a chunk of time devoted to celebrating these life moments. We eat big portions of the best foods and laugh. And then we live the rest of the year, in between the profoundness of these moments.

I can't help but think God enjoys throwing parties well. Scripture tells us that there is more rejoicing in Heaven over one sinner who repents than ninety-nine righteous people who do not need to. There is celebrating in Heaven. Does that mean dancing, food, and drink? Does that mean Heaven is like a party?

Several times in the gospels, Heaven is described as a wedding feast. It is said to be a table full of food and drink that can seat many guests. Culturally, a Jewish wedding feast was an epic celebration. It ran a week long at times, involving family, friends, and a community. Working with youth, we've often talked about following a God who likes to party. We've talked about the differences between God's parties and the ones we find ourselves invited to in high school. There has even been a few times where we threw parties at church. We had lights and music, and people danced. We laughed and made memories and reminded one another that Heaven is going to be a party.

There is a nursing home a few blocks away from our church. It's rundown, dirty, and not a place anyone would like to spend their free time at. But our church has seen it as a place to serve and love. We have a number of members who live here and we desire to make it a better place. We've done projects and fundraisers; we've played bingo and walked dogs with the residents, but the greatest gift we give them every year is a party.

Most of the residents there don't have family to come and visit them. Things can get incredibly lonely around the holidays. Sometimes family members drop them off here and don't come back; other times, people just get busy and forget to stop by. Christmas is especially difficult. So we devised a plan…every Christmas, we throw a party for the residents. The party is complete with food and dessert, and every resident gets a present to open. We take down their requests, and people buy them a present and bring it on this day. The last couple of years, we even had a stand-in Santa there. They seemed to like Santa, and they tell us everything is great—the food, the presents, the decorations, but they always request one final component for their parties: dancing.

Men and women, many of whom spend most of their waking hours sitting in a chair or lying in bed, get on the dance floor. The spirit of life is in their eyes as they sway back and forth to the music. They smile, laugh and invite others to join in. Some of them practically dance the entire party away.

I love going to the Christmas party. I love dancing and seeing happiness in the eyes of the forgotten and excluded. I love that a good party is possible anywhere. I am overwhelmed when I realize that God intends for us to celebrate life and to celebrate it often. I am aware now, more than ever, that we are moving from the grasp of this world into the open embrace of our true home. Partying is just the beginning. I am reminded that God tells us to throw parties not just for our friends, but for people who can never pay us back.

God invites us to change the definition of who our neighbor is. He calls us to share from our table because we are celebrating life together. Together. The party begins now and continues to the next side. Perhaps the more we celebrate, the clearer picture we get of what God is like—a God who is for weddings and parties; a God who says this is what Heaven is like.

As we develop eyes to see *beyond*, we see why parties are an integral part of the spiritual life. A party, after all, is a chance to be caught *in between.*

Beyoncé Has a Bodyguard

I used to think life was divided between insiders and outsiders. Now I know: God sees things differently.

My friend Matt has grown up around movie sets his entire life. His dad works on movies, music videos, and commercials, and Matt has been privy to all sorts of cool stuff that comes with the territory—meeting celebrities, being an extra in a Justin Timberlake music video, and even starring in a few roles himself. I've always been fascinated by Hollywood, and so when he asked if I wanted to hang out one day on the set of a music video, I was ecstatic. Part of me didn't even care who the artist was; just the opportunity to go was enough for me. Matt told me it was a music video for Beyoncé

"Beyoncé and I are friends," I told him.

"Really?" he asked, because when you live in LA, you never

know.

"No, I lied," I said. "She used to wear jean overalls and rap about waterfalls, right?"

"TLC is not the same thing as Destiny's Child," he said.

Anyway, one day we drove to a studio in Burbank where the music video was being filmed. Turns out, most movie sets are not that glamorous. This particular studio was a couple of warehouses connected together by large hangar doors and slabs of concrete (of course, Hollywood can make magic happen regardless of where you're at). Once inside the studios, we met different people from the business. We talked with some and even shared a meal together. There was a catering truck, plus tables of all kinds of snacks. Lots of people were walking around frantically, smoking cigarettes and drinking coffee and pacing. There was lots of pacing.

I tried to act like I was someone there for a job. I paced around a bit too, sipping my coffee and incessantly looking down at my phone. I even thought about making up a phony resume or seeing if there was anyway I could create an IMDB account and boast of my on screen appearances. Matt pretended like he didn't know me.

Eventually, we made it onto the actual set where the filming was happening and where Matt's dad was working. It's fascinating how many people were working on this one music video. There were copious amounts of camera guys and people carrying around long cables and gigantic lights. Then there were choreographers, directors, and—of course—Beyoncé. She's actually much taller in real life, about seven feet I think. (Okay, she wasn't that tall.) Matt and I sat on the side, a few feet outside of the camera shot, and watched. I assume we looked like we didn't belong there because a very large and in charge fellow kept scowling over at us. He was roughly the size of a semi truck and had an uncanny resemblance to Deebo from the *Friday* movies.[25] I waved at him, and he kept staring my way.

We found out soon enough he had a massively important job—

he was Beyoncé's bodyguard. It was weird seeing someone actually have a bodyguard in real life. I thought that stuff was only in the movies, but this guy was not acting. He was working and making sure no one got too close to her.

As the night progressed, more and more people started filtering in to watch the music video. Beyoncé's bodyguard became a little antsy. I don't know why, but he stared over at Matt and me and told us to leave. And then after telling us to leave, he got up and escorted us out. Just like that, the music video was now a closed set and if you didn't belong, you were out. I waved goodbye to Beyoncé as I left. She didn't wave back, and Matt shook his head in shame.

My time on this Hollywood set reminded me that life is often an experience of being on the inside or the outside—almost as if there are bodyguards letting certain people in and keeping others out. This is how the world works. Certain individuals are the accepted ones, the included ones, and then there are others who are on the fringes, looking to find a way inside. Our lives operate like this, even from the time we're little, and it continues well into adulthood.

Have you ever noticed that when people talk about junior high or high school, they do so in relation to being an insider or an outsider? Those of us who had a great time in high school were usually the ones who were on the inside—part of the popular crowd, on the football team, or dated the prom queen. Some of us were star athletes or had money, or had some kind of fame or notoriety. We were the cool version of Ronald Miller in *Can't Buy Me Love*.[26]

On the other hand, if we were on the fringes of the high school social scene, our school memories might not be as cheery. Reminiscing of high school might actually be painful because it brings back the very real feelings of being rejected and ostracized.

To make matters worse, this dynamic of inside or outside is constantly communicated to us. We are reminded that we are on the outside, trying to get in. We keep spending money to make us worthy of moving to the inside. We have surgeries, spending umpteen amounts of money to have the perfect physique. Like addicts, we consume infomercials and soak in all of Dr. Phil and Dr. Oz's propaganda, resulting in overpriced books, juicers, and God forbid, a shake weight. Perhaps we start to wonder, though, if this is all just a sham.

One of the most compelling things about Jesus is that He understood this inside/outside dynamic and lived to correct it. He purposefully spent time with the "inside religious crowd" and also those society deemed as "outsiders": the poor, the morally bankrupt, the marginalized, those on the fringes of society. He did this unapologetically and began to break down barriers that society had erected to maintain the status quo. He did this, and it was beautiful. He reminded us that people are lost both on the inside and the outside, and insiders and outsiders both desperately need God.

The gospel writer Luke tells a few beautiful stories that illustrate this insider/outsider dynamic. Luke 15 is a collection of three parables centered on the theme of being lost. The first story concerns a shepherd who has lost a sheep. Out of the hundred sheep he owns, he is willing to leave ninety-nine behind to search for the one that wandered away from the fold. This one sheep has become lost, separated from the herd. The sheep—literally and symbolically— is lost on the outside, and the shepherd searches for this one lost sheep at the expense of leaving the others behind, and then he rejoices when it is found.

The next story is of a lady who loses a coin. This coin means a great deal to her. Many commentators speculate the coin represents close to a year's income. So, she does exactly as we would do if we lost a lot of money: She searches every nook and cranny of her house. Again, there is much rejoicing because something that was lost is now found. She had lost the coin inside her house. Outside. Inside. Two ways that something can be lost. And that leads us to the largest story in chapter 15—the story of the lost son.

Most of us are at least familiar with this one. Much thought and words have been committed to understanding this story. The famous Renaissance painter Rembrandt captured it in one of his paintings, and Christian theologian Henri Nouwen wrote about the story and how Rembrandt's painting of the story influenced his own understanding of it.

The Cliffnotes: A father has two sons. One day, the younger son asks his father for his inheritance, which turns out to be a pretty messed up thing to do. It's kind of like shaking the cards you get on your birthday, to see if they have money in them, and then only caring if they do. Except it's even worse because to ask for an inheritance early would be like saying to your old man, "You're dead to me. All I care about is getting my paper. Make it rain, Pop-pop; make it rain." The father grants the son's request and gives him the money due him.

Next, the son goes off to a far away land and begins to live the life of a high roller. He echoes that Black Eyed Peas' song "I Gotta a Feeling," and is sure to "spend it up." The text tells us he spent it on "wild living." Perhaps he spent it on fast cars and slow women or slow cars and fast women. Either way, he lives it up and spends his money to the point where he is broke. All of a sudden, he has nothing left in his pockets and is searching for work in a town that is far away from his home. He finds employment tending pigs, a very unrespectable job as a Jewish person. Things have gotten so bad that it doesn't matter though. He even longs to eat the slop the pigs have.

It's quite the turn of events, and Luke adds these details so we know just how bad it's gotten for this young man. He goes from being in the limelight to having nothing at all, becoming a person on the bottom rung of the ladder of success. He is merely a day laborer at this point, at the end of his rope, living alone, broken, and poor. But then he has an epiphany. He remembers how good it was at his father's place. His father has servants, and they have it better than he does. He should return home and tell his father that he messed up and perhaps, then, his father will agree to let him be a servant. At least he'll have something to eat this way.

So he heads home. Being a long way off, his father sees him and runs to him (Luke 15: 20). Henri Nouwen calls this the most beautiful verse in the Bible.[27] The father, running towards his lost, beat-up son, throws his arms around him, kisses him, and throws him a welcome home party. The son can't even squeak out his well-rehearsed speech before the father interrupts him. It is a beautiful picture of the love of God and His forgiveness. But something else is happening in the story as well. We forget there is another son, the eldest child. He is the good son—the one who stayed behind and didn't insult his father or make a mockery of the family. He was the faithful son. And he is livid.

The older son yells at this father, asking why this tomfoolery, why a party for this "son" of his. He is so angry he can't even call him his brother. The father reassures his son that all the father has is his, but they had to celebrate his brother coming home.

The story ends with this tension, as good stories often do. Some have said this story should really be called the "Parable of the Lost Sons." Both the older brother and younger brother are lost. The younger is lost on the outside while the older is lost on the inside.

It is a perfect illustration for the segregated society of Jesus' day. The religious leaders, those on the inside, were just as lost as those forced to the outside. Jesus came not to appease insiders and rebuke outsiders; rather, He came to unite the two groups, to show us there is no such thing as a family in which some of God's children are accepted and others are not. And yet, thousands of years later, we continue to live this way to an even larger degree. Moreover, the sad, unfortunate, and inconvenient truth is that the church is not leading the way. We are simply following in suit to the example of our world.

Our churches have grown bigger and flashier. We've built mega corporations and figured out a way to create a system that celebrates those who are on the inside. Our homogeneous units boast of numbers and most of us in our churches look the same, act the same, and worship the same. We've done plenty to help those in need through the giving of money and special work projects, but we have done little to include the same people we help on Sunday mornings. We stand around in our churches like bodyguards, seeing who belongs and who needs to go.

It's like that scene in the movie *Sabrina* where Audrey Hepburn says life is like a limousine.[28] There are those who sit behind the glass and those who drive the limousine. In other words, there is the one percent, the insiders, and then there are those who live on the fringes. There is a glass barrier separating the two, and it cannot be crossed. Sadly, some people live this lie and echo this dichotomy with their actions and words. But not Jesus.

Jesus told stories of the poor, outcasts, sinners, and the righteous being together at the same table. He was accused of being a drunkard and glutton and eating at the house of sinners. This dynamic is called social solidarity—equality existing in a society full of segregation. He lives his life in such a way that societal lines of division were blurred. While reading Christ's teaching, we are reminded we have incongruous identity in the Father.

Shel Silverstein understood something about the importance of inclusion. I love his poem, *An Invitation*:

> If you are a dreamer, come in
> If you are a dreamer, a wisher, a liar
> A hope-er, a pray-er, a magic bean buyer
> If you're a pretender, come sit by my fire,
> For we have some flax golden tales to spin
> Come in!
> Come in!

I'm not sure what Silverstein intended with this poem, but it makes me think about the inclusive nature of God. I imagine Heaven is like God sitting by a campfire, listening to us tell Him stories. He is like a wise old man who has seen the world and is well read. He pokes the fire with a stick and sips black coffee from a thermos. He strokes a long grey beard and has a hearty laugh that shakes His body from His head to His toes. He sits by this campfire and watches the horizon to see if anyone is approaching. I imagine Him echoing the words of Shel Silverstein, inviting anyone and everyone to come sit by His fire and share stories of life on earth. I imagine Him just asking questions and listening to us talk for hours. When I begin to feel self-conscious or nervous about some of the things I've done on earth, He has this kind demeanor like a grandfather who knows that His time with me is precious so He only focuses on the important stuff.

I also imagine there will be more people around the campfire than not. I bet I see faces of people I met on earth. There will be people seated around that campfire that I wouldn't expect to be there. God will say to them with the same kindness He says to us all, "Come in." His words will echo for eternity, and we will breathe deep in His presence. Slowly, but surely, we will realize there is no inside or outside in His presence. There are no bodyguards. There is just an empty chair and a God who waits for us to come and join Him by the fire.

Living *in between* is like that—it's realizing that God is for all people.

Ecuadorian Hospitality

God has a different view of family and reminds us there is always room at His table.

Recently, I've started to notice the significance of sharing a meal with someone. There is something special happening when we share food and drink and invite others to our table. We open up our pantries and give nourishment, but we also open up our lives and give of ourselves. The entire process is quite intimate. When I share a meal with someone, our relationship goes to another level.

I love the image of an infinitely open door and an extra seat at my table. I often joke with people at our church during different meals and gatherings that there will always be room for someone to come and sit, eat and drink. We've become adept at adding chairs and squeezing as many people as possible around a table. An open table is a great illustration of the Christian life, because living like Jesus is an invitation to show reckless hospitality; it's about squeezing as many people around your table as possible, and bringing out food and drink for all to share.

I discovered the importance of an open table during a trip to Ecuador one summer. I quickly learned how giving and welcoming the Ecuadorian people are, and also how quickly you become family to them.

During our stay, we took a couple of days to visit a small town on the beach called Curia. It was a quaint town with unpaved roads, small buildings, and ramshackle houses running through it. Children played barefoot in the muddy streets, and adults sat in plastic chairs on street corners sipping cokes from glass bottles. It only took a few minutes to walk through the entire town. And it was beautiful. You could hear the ocean crash upon the shore, and the air smelled of the sea.

We stayed the weekend with a couple named Carlos and Jeanette. Carlos was a native Ecuadorian and his wife, Jeanette, was from Georgia. They had been married for a number of years, and most of their lives had been spent in the States. Now, Carlos and Jeanette were both retired, and they decided to move to Ecuador for their golden years. They had an incredible house that sat right on the beach on the edge of town. It was a three-story house with views of the ocean no matter where you stood. Carlos had built the house a few years earlier, making trips back and forth from Georgia to Ecuador to supervise the construction and progress. I soon learned Carlos had a lot to teach us.

There was a reason behind building the big house Carlos and Jeanette retired in. The second floor of the home was full of bunk beds and extra bedrooms. Carlos and Jeanette host teams from the States and have them help with different projects in the town. That night our group stayed in this big house right on the beach. I was learning something about what it meant to give and to welcome someone into your house. Carlos was constantly serving us, asking if we needed anything.

As we made dinner that night, Carlos invited a man named Sebastian from town to join us. Sebastian had been coming to a weekly church service put on by Carlos and his wife, and he was now in their home eating dinner with us. He was given a chance to speak towards the end of the meal. He spoke in Spanish, and one of our team members translated. He talked about how his faith in God led him to family. He felt welcomed. He felt like he belonged. His transformation and the change he experienced in his life was linked to the hospitality of those around him.

That night we sat out on Carlos's porch and listened to the sound of the ocean. Jeanette made us tea, and we sat, sipping the tea, staring out into the darkness of the ocean. I could remember so many nights in California that I'd spent staring into the same ocean. I used to love to walk down the pier at Huntington Beach and just stare out into the darkness of the Pacific. I always wondered who else was doing it too, in another part of the world. I felt a connection that night realizing people around the globe were doing the same thing.

When Carlos spoke, he called us sons and daughters. His voice was hearty and full, and by his presence alone you felt safe. He was like a wise sage, a timeless grandfather whose wrinkles on his face were the years of wisdom he'd accumulated. He asked questions about us, engaged and excited by what we had to say. I listened as a guy on our team described his love of hardcore music, and Carlos thought that sounded delightful. We stayed up late that night. We poured more tea and laughed. We felt like we had known each other longer than just a few hours.

The next morning, Carlos loaded us up in the back of his jeep. We drove down the beach, with the wind blowing in our hair. Carlos smiled as we enjoyed the view. He drove us into town. He showed us the community center they were developing for local kids and adults. He took us by a local school and introduced us to the principal. We were in his town, and we were honored guests to everyone we met. Next, Carlos drove up a hill and showed us more of his land. He had horses, goats, and a colossal pig that he was afraid to name in case they needed to send him to the butcher. Carlos enjoyed farming, but he also enjoyed employing people to work on his farm and making money to give away.

After we spent some time on the farm, Carlos drove us down the hill. You could see the town in the distance, with the ocean behind it. I saw Carlos smile as we headed back to town. He looked at me and said, "This is my home." I understood what that meant to call something your home. This wasn't his temporary dwelling place, nor was this a vacation spot. This was home. Carlos talked about a young couple who was moving to Curia to partner with him in their work. He had been looking for a house to buy them because, he said, "When you have a home, it feels permanent."

That afternoon, we packed our bags and prepared to leave. We stood outside, took a couple of pictures from the balcony, and were genuinely saddened to go. Carlos placed his big hands around us and said, "You became family so quickly." We got in our cars and stared up at the balcony of the house. Carlos and Jeanette waved and blew us kisses as we drove away, with Curia in the background and our new family sending us off. My time in Ecuador has stayed with me. Over the years, I continue to process what it means to be family and to build community.

When I first moved to Los Angeles several years ago, I had this one neighbor named Tony. He had a fairly rough exterior. He always wore a fisherman's hat, had a long grey Duck-Dynasty beard, and was always smoking something. He used to sit out on his porch at night and watch the streetlights come on. We lived in this little house that was not in the greatest neighborhood. Our car got broken into, and we had some gang activity that was close by. Nevertheless, I always felt safe having Tony next door.

Tony was always on the lookout for anything suspicious, and he was the kind of guy that would come knock on your door if you left your car light on. I remembered feeling sad when we moved and said goodbye to each other. I wanted to take Tony with me and have him be my permanent neighbor. I told him thanks for everything over the years, and all he said was, "I was just being a neighbor."

Jesus talks about the importance of being neighborly and practicing hospitality. His words challenge us to think about whom we invite to our table and what our attitude should be towards everyone we meet. Jesus tells this story in the gospel of Luke about a wedding feast.[29] The story goes: there was a king who throws a wedding feast and invites his entire kingdom. He sends out a plethora of invitations, but no one can make the event. They make excuses. They are too busy to enjoy this feast. So, in rather dramatic fashion, the king calls his servants to go and invite people off the streets—the poor, the crippled, the blind. He fills his banquet with people who would normally not be invited. The original guests invited to the wedding miss out on what was prepared. In Matthew's version, the story ends with Jesus saying, "Many are called, but few are chosen."[30]

This story makes me think about what it means to be invited. It makes me think about hospitality—and how, so often, we are only comfortable inviting the people like us. I've heard that following Jesus is a life of radical hospitality, but we've failed to put that into practice. We keep thinking the original guests will show up. I often wonder if maybe we're inviting the wrong people. Maybe our focus is too narrow and specific. We need to realize that family is a lot closer than we might think.

I often think about my time in Ecuador. Every once in a while, I find myself slowing down and remembering that night on Carlos' and Jeanette's balcony. I remember the way the breeze felt in my hair. I can recall the words Carlos said. I remember the feeling of being home, even though I had just arrived. When Carlos and Jeanette said goodbye to us from their balcony, I remember a final word Carlos said to us. He yelled out as we drove down his street, "See you soon, or see you in Heaven."

I'm starting to see that the family you make here is going to be there. The wedding feast we're invited to here is only going to get bigger. Jesus reminds us there is always room at His table. Perhaps we need to rethink who are our brothers and sisters, mothers and fathers. In John 19, Jesus is dying on the cross and there before Him is His mother, Mary, and His closest friend, John. Jesus speaks to them both, telling John that Mary is now his mother and to Mary that John is now her son. It's a nice sentiment for sure—a few kind words and condolences to people He cared about. But Jesus was actually doing something extraordinary. He expands the meaning of family. No longer will family simply be what you can trace on your family tree. Now, by the blood Jesus shed on the cross, a new family has been created.

The family we make here is going to be there. Hospitality is close to the heart of God. There is always room at God's table, just like there is always room in our lives for more family. When we learn to see *beyond*, and learn to live *in between,* family takes on a new meaning.

Gardens and Garage Sales

Christianity has never been about what you don't do. Following Jesus is about living as He lived and doing what He did.

Theologian and commentator guru John Stott once said, "Every claim to love God is a delusion if it is not accompanied by unselfish and practical love for our brothers and sisters."[31] This delusion, according to Stott, is what happens when we take this Christian life, this desire to follow Jesus, and we refuse or withhold it instead of living with His love towards others. What we have is an unrecognizable existence.

Love shows itself by action. It is an obvious sentiment, but how often do we forget this one foundational component of love? More often than not, our faith is not about what we do. Rather our faith has become merely a classification to identify with. Yes, I have faith and religion and morals, but you wouldn't be able to tell that by how I lived. The New Testament writer John says this kind of faith is false. Fake. Our inability to love one another grants us the title of liar (1 John 4:20).

A couple years ago, I awoke one Saturday morning to my ringing cell phone. It was a pastor from our church. He told me there was an older woman in our community named June who was evicted from her place and needed a last minute garage sale to make money to help with the move. June needed willing people to help her set up and run the garage sale, and it was going to start in an hour. Now, I usually treat my Saturday mornings like something set apart and holy, typically operating with unapologetic indifference when someone attempts to interrupt them. But that didn't happen this morning. Something tugged on my heart, so I grabbed my phone and sent a group text message. "Kingdom Opportunity. Serve someone in need. Meet at 8:00am at church." That was it. And people showed up.

We walked over to her house, which happened to be only a few blocks away from our church. June lived in a small duplex that was packed wall to wall with a lifetime of collected memories and knick-knacks. She told us that all of it had to go, so we began to pack up her things and set them out on the lawn in front of her house. It didn't take long for us to get to know June and hear her story. She kept thanking us for what I believed was an infinitesimally small gesture, and yet it meant the world to her.

We laid tarps on the ground and gently separated her things into various piles. We stacked books, folded clothes, and arranged her plates and pans neatly. Before we finished setting up, people were already arriving, eager to buy her things. As most garage sales go, people bartered with us about the prices we had given the items. It was funny because we fought our customers if they gave us a price that was too low. During the course of the morning, we had forgotten whose stuff this was. We wanted to get the best price we could. One high school girl who came to help us with the sale was the boldest of us all. She wouldn't take no for an answer and turned into an auctioneer with the verbal speed of Busta Ryhmes.

Our group worked on the garage sale all morning until most of her things were sold and she had a shoebox full of cash. I noticed at one point during the morning June was crying. My heart went out to her. I've never been in a position where I was forced to sell everything I owned just to make it. I imagined the pain she must have felt to let go of her things, especially those with sentimental value. I approached her and told her I was sorry this was happening. I told her I was sorry she was losing her house and her things. I tried to console her in some way.

Eventually, June wiped her eyes and stared into mine. She said she wasn't crying over selling her things or losing her house. Her tears weren't tears of sadness or pain. Rather, she said she cried out of happiness, because there existed a group of people who were willing to help someone they didn't know.

Standing there, I thought about her words. It was true—we didn't know each other, but in another way, we did. History has proven me to be quite taciturn, particularly in situations where I don't know the person that well. But for some reason, I couldn't hold back. With the same determined glance that June shot my way, I responded in turn. "We're not strangers…and we're not even neighbors. We're more than that. We're family." And family shows up on Saturdays to help with garage sales.

Around the same time we helped June, we had an opportunity to share love with a few other people in our community. In the city where we live, there are quite a few retirement communities. A number of these residents come to our church on Sunday. They walk over together in a long line of walkers and wheelchairs. We have fun when they're around. Often times they are loud and yell out things during service, ignoring any typical church decorum that states we should behave like kids at the family gathering—seen, but not heard. It's kind of funny because their outbursts are what everyone is thinking, but just too nervous to say out loud. I like that someone else does that for me.

Over the years we've done a few projects at the retirement homes, trying our best to be like Jesus and love all people, even the ones our society has turned their backs on. So, we got together one spring and decided to do something. We weren't sure at first what we wanted to do; we just knew we needed to act. What came out of a few meetings and conversations was a plan to build a garden.

We discovered there was this outdoor space that connected the dorms at the retirement home. However, the space was dirty and dilapidated. If they had a gardener, he hadn't been around that decade. The outdoor area was full of old cigarette butts, trash, and dirt. It's hard to enjoy an outdoor space when it's polluted, and we believed the people deserved a beautiful garden because they were beautiful too. So, we got to work. We put in trees and plants and flowers. We swept up the trash and cigarette butts. We hosed down the grounds and cleaned the windows so people could feel the sun shine into their rooms. We fixed an old broken fountain, allowing a water feature to be present. We hung wind chimes all over the garden so music would echo constantly. We got our hands dirty making something beautiful out of a place that had decayed over time.

One of our volunteers that day was a young kid named Rob. You probably know his story because it is universal. He's mad at his family, mad at the world, and looking for attention, so he acts out. He drinks. He smokes. He fights. He looks for ways to be destructive. This is the same kid that tagged our church, stole from other students in the youth group, and came very close to going to jail a number of times. I don't know why, but he showed up the day we helped out at the retirement center. He got down on his hands and knees to plant roses. He talked to residents and served them pastries and juice. I wasn't sure what was happening with him, but something in his heart was changing.

It's amazing how loving others reminds us of what it means to love ourselves. When we serve the less fortunate, we begin to see with new eyes and often times take account of what we're doing with our time. It's crazy, but we can't be involved in community and service and step out unchanged.

Much of our time and energy is spent trying to figure out how to attract people to what we do. It makes sense. We all want to be liked and accepted in the same way that we want to be validated and affirmed. But we can forget the life that Jesus modeled for us was a simple life. He told us to love one another. And the truth of God's love makes sense when it is lived out. When we're willing to step out of the walls that surround us—out of comfort and predictability—we position ourselves to change the trajectory of our lives and communities.

In John's gospel, Jesus shares a brief thought, inserted within a larger context of sharing what will happen to His followers after He's gone. In two short verses, He gives them a command that is clear and to the point. "A new command I give you: Love one another. As I have loved you, so you must love one another. By this everyone will know that you are my disciples, if you love one another" (John 13:34-35). Jesus says our greatest testimony to the reality of God is when we love one another. How do we defend Christianity? How do we develop the right apologetic to win arguments and disprove doubters? I don't know. Perhaps God doesn't need a defense, but an offense. It's true. The incontrovertible and undeniable evidence that Jesus is alive and well in the world, is when His followers choose to love one another.

When we have garage sales and build gardens we may be closer to the heart of God than we ever imagined. When we choose to practically love and serve those around us we are shouting to a dark world that light is here. Truth has come. It is revealed in spoken words, but also lived out in tangible ways. There's no such thing as being strangers in this world. We are children, united by the same Father who came that we might know a love that heals the world. The more we love, the more we realize this love is changing us, one person at a time. When we love like that, we experience the joy of being caught *in between;* we taste what it means to experience Heaven on Earth.

Wrestling Rings and Fireworks

Jesus invites us to take risks. Faith, in part, is going where we've never gone before.

When I was in college, I worked at a church plant for a couple of years. We were in the process of getting a building to meet in, but in the meantime, we met at an Elks Lodge in downtown Santa Ana. I'm not sure if you're familiar with the Elk's. I really wasn't. I just remember the lodge was massive, and there were deer heads in every room and also big portraits of creepy old white guys who were obviously important for some reason. We met with our junior high students in a big room with chairs like bleachers and plenty of deer heads and oversized portraits. Admittedly, it was kind of a cool thing. I was leading worship with an acoustic guitar inside an Elk's Lodge off the 5 freeway. And we had a lot of fun in those days.

I didn't go at this gig solo, but partnered with a good friend of mine. In time, we developed the perfect system for college students who stayed up too late on Saturday nights. We'd alternate week by week who got the first shower Sunday morning. One person showered, and the other made coffee. Then we were on the freeway heading south to Santa Ana. We'd spend the car ride rehearsing our set list and warming up our vocals. Once at the lodge, we got more coffee and a doughnut and went over our songs before the students arrived.

I remember one Sunday where everything started off normal, but then took an unexpected turn. My alarm went off like every Sunday, and I forced myself out of bed to take the first shower. Twenty minutes later, we got in my car and headed to the Elk's Lodge.

We grabbed our coffee and doughnuts and made our way to the auditorium. Then we turned the lights on in the room with bleacher seats, and we saw it. Inside our auditorium was a full-size wrestling ring. You know, the kind Macho Man Randy Savage and Hulk Hogan would go to battle in. Yep. Right smack in the middle of our auditorium was a wrestling ring. Church plants can be a lot of fun.

What's interesting is we didn't receive any warning the week before. There wasn't a note or sign stating, "Next week, there will be a wrestling ring in your meeting space. Don't worry. Have fun"— signed creepy white guys from the Elk's Lodge. Nope. Nothing. Zilch. Nada. I remember standing there with my guitar in hand looking at the ring and wondering how we'd make it work. We couldn't just ignore this massive eyesore where we usually set up to lead worship. So, we decided to go with it. We ran around inside the wrestling ring and bounced off the ropes. I tried to mimic some of the wrestlers I used to see on television. I said stuff like, "Do you know what I'm cooking?!" and, "It's time for some sweet chin music." I summoned the collective spirits of the Rock and Brett Michaels.[32]

When our students showed up that morning, they were surprised to see us set up inside a wrestling ring. It was actually one of the coolest days we had at that Elk's Lodge. We came to church expecting one thing, and we're surprised by something all together different, like a giant wrestling ring with two college guys who looked nothing like wrestlers. Sometimes expectations are smashed to pieces. And sometimes something beautiful arises from the rubble. We led worship inside a wrestling ring that morning. Maybe it was irreverent, but mostly it was fun and memorable.

A couple years ago my wife and I volunteered at a local fireworks stand on the Fourth of July. We sold fireworks to help raise money for teenagers to go to summer camp. Our shift ended at 8:00pm, so we locked up our firework stand and tried to find a place in our city to watch fireworks. Unfortunately, we were too late to find parking at the local high school where every year they attempt to blow up the city with patriotic enthusiasm. We'd spent the entire day inside a metal booth selling fireworks, so we were sort of defeated, wishing we could do something fun.

We drove by a few places where we could watch fireworks, but it was no use. If you've ever lived in LA, then you know traffic and parking are dance partners in the land of suck. Eventually, though, we drove by our church, and I had an idea: what if we create our own venue to watch fireworks? Without hesitating, we ran inside. After raiding the kitchen for a couple juice boxes, two bags of chips and licorice, we accessed the roof. We put two chairs down and faced our local high school.

Leaning back, we sipped our juice boxes just as the firework show began. The sky directly above us became filled with colors of red, white, and blue. The fireworks cracked and boomed in the sky, shaking our plastic folding chairs on the roof that night. Music blared and filled our ears, and we realized something through it all: we had the best seats in the city for the show. I'll never forget how we took a typical Fourth of July and made it extraordinary. A beautiful experience unfolded that evening. It was something hidden and unexpected that proved to be one of the more memorable Fourth of July celebrations I've ever had.

When moments like this happen, I'm reminded that our lives are full of opportunities to make the most of any situation. At times it may be as simple as breaking out of the ordinary. We can call it risk, or stepping out of our comfort zone, but whatever we call it, the palpable truth is we choose what we do with the time given us. I'm starting to learn life is most beautiful when you're not expecting anything. This way, you can be sure to live with open arms and receive whatever comes your way. Sometimes, in order to live this kind of unhindered existence, we have to be willing to break the rules—especially if the rules set in place are by people who have no business making them.

In Matthew 5, there's a section of Scripture called the Sermon on the Mount where Jesus, the greatest teacher who ever lived, preaches the greatest sermon ever uttered.[33] He climbs a mountain to give a word, just like Moses climbed Mount Sinai years before to receive God's word in the form of the Ten Commandments. The symbolism is undeniable. Now Jesus gives His word, fulfilling the law that came before Him.

Through the course of this message, Jesus shares a few rather pointed and severe words of criticisms to certain members of the crowd. His harshest words are directed at the Pharisees. "Do not think I've come to abolish the law and the prophets. I have not come to abolish them, but to fulfill them," He says.

Now, the Pharisees were known for "being good." They had figured out a way to live the law like no one else. But in doing so, they'd juxtaposed their own man-made, religious traditions next to God's law. Instead of reflecting the heart of His commandments— God's disposition for mercy and compassion—they'd created a legalistic checklist to decide who was on God's side. Essentially, their laws and traditions decreed, "Do this and you're in; do that and you're out." Jesus saw through their hypocrisy and accused these religious bureaucrats of doing away with the true meaning of the law.

Jesus rejects the man-made procedures of his day—the false

law and traditions—and instead seeks God's original intention. The law was never meant to be more about regulations than character. Jesus gets that. In fact, He understands this more than anyone ever has before because He knows the unique role He plays in completing the law. He uses an authoritative principle no one else has used this far in Scripture—Himself. The law was merely a shadow of what was to come. It pointed all along to its greater fulfillment. Jesus becomes the interpretive key to the entire Bible. He is the lens with which we see everything. If we want to know God, we stay close to Jesus. The more we read about Jesus, we see how He constantly gave people a new vision of God. Often times this would come about in his unique teachings and revelation about God. He'd say, "You think God is like this; let me show you what God is truly like."

Even in our culture today, a lot of people have a misunderstanding of who Jesus is and what the church is called to be. Christians from all places get lumped in with a few examples that make headlines. It's the egregious, prosperity gospel TV preacher wearing his Rolex and riding around in his private jet. Or the befuddled lunatics picketing and screaming their hate messages. Either way, Jesus gets a bad rap, and we're left picking up the pieces from someone else's mess.

It's not fair. It's not easy. Sometimes I want to crawl underground and wait it out. And yet, there is an opportunity. Perhaps we can go as far as to say we live in a time and place with unprecedented opportunities to give the world a shocking and serendipitous experience when it comes to God. What if instead of settling for what has always been or complaining about how someone misrepresented God, we choose to respond in new, life-giving ways. What if we choose to break the mundane with the truth of the God who is alive and active.

Perhaps God isn't concerned with crossing the t's and dotting the i's as much as He is concerned with you and me experiencing a relationship with Him. Following God is going to be about risks and chances. It's an experience in breaking the rules. It's about doing something new and finding truth where before there was confusion. The church needs to be willing to break the rules the way Jesus broke the rules. The church needs to be willing to go with the punches, smashing expectations and surprising the world in unique and beautiful ways.

I'll never forget this one Sunday at our church where our senior pastor was preaching on love. During the middle of his sermon, a woman who was agitated for some reason and had not gone through the whole church decorum class—aka, this is how you act during church—decided to speak up. She actually started to debate with the pastor during the sermon. She yelled out loud, "I have a question. Can you answer my question?"

There were several hundred people in the church that day, but you could have heard a pin drop. I found myself standing up, preparing to move towards the front to help escort the woman out of the room. She kept talking loudly during the sermon. Now, if you've ever done any preaching or public speaking, you know how difficult it can be to deal with an agitated and argumentative audience member. It throws off your whole sermon vibe, and you lose your train of thought.

Our pastor responded differently than most. He didn't stand up on the stage and make a big deal about her interrupting his sermon or anything like that. He didn't take umbrage at her behavior. He spoke lovingly to her. He stopped his message and just spoke to her like she was a child of God because she was and then continued his sermon. It was the greatest sermon he'd ever preached, and no one in that church forgot it.

I remember one night during our youth service a homeless lady came in through the front doors. She was wearing all black and smelled foul. She pushed a shopping cart into our worship center and sat down in the front room. It was a test for a room full of high school students. But one by one they welcomed this lady, got her a drink, and helped her feel welcome. It was a response I didn't expect, and it was beautiful.

When Jesus tells us to love one another the way He loved us, he's inviting us to be different. When the world expects hate, we bring love. When the world seeks judgment and condemnation, we offer exoneration and freedom. When the world laughs at the downtrodden and pokes fun at those who are different, the church says, "We belong together; come inside the Father's house. There is plenty of room for all."

Sometimes we need to break the rules. Sometimes we need to surprise the world with the hope and love of a God who is present with us now, beckoning us to know Him more. Expectations can be smashed. God brings clarity even in confusion. He brings truth in the chaos. He makes good out of bad. Let's trust Him to take risks and change what needs to be changed. Let's observe with renewed eyes, focused on seeing *in between.* If that happens, we'll be willing to break the rules every once in a while.

Act III Echoes of Heaven

"I have come home at last! This is my real country! I belong here. This is the land I have been looking for all my life, though I never knew it till now...Come further up, come further in!"
— C.S. Lewis, The Last Battle

"Then I saw 'a new heaven and a new earth, '[a] for the first heaven and the first earth had passed away, and there was no longer any sea. ² I saw the Holy City, the new Jerusalem, coming down out of heaven from God, prepared as a bride beautifully dressed for her husband." Revelation 21:1-2

Life is full to the brim of signs that Heaven is coming here. It's people we meet and the events that occur that are overt and subtle reminders of the new life that is available. It's here, and it's slowly coming into fruition.

What Grandma Tiny Knew

The life of Jesus was about the radical acceptance of all people. Jesus knew people and called them by name. A name matters.

Every once in a while, you meet someone who is so life giving and influential that you can't help but rethink life itself when you're around them. People like this are rare and when you meet someone whose soul burns bright, you can't help but leave changed. One of these characters in my life was a little elderly lady aptly named Grandma Tiny.

Grandma Tiny was known by this incredible epithet because she was indeed tiny. I mean small. Minuscule in size. She only stood about four-foot eight inches and weighed maybe seventy pounds. But her heart made up for her lack of height. I knew her when she was in her late nineties. You'd see her around church on a Sunday, slowly meandering through campus. She'd constantly tell me that she'd lost all her teeth. And I'd tell her that was okay; she was still beautiful. The more time I spent around Grandma Tiny, the clearer it became she knew something most of us had forgotten.

Every Sunday, you'd find her slowly making her way around our café. She'd greet everyone present, even people she didn't know. Deliberately, she walked around the campus, giving hugs, kisses, and the constant word of appreciation. It wasn't uncommon to see her hugging people and holding their face in her hands. She'd stare deeply into their eyes like she was gazing at the true part of them. She'd tell them how proud she was of who they are. She'd kiss them and tell them how cute they were as babies. As her greeting marathon came to an end, she'd slowly head out to find her seat at church.

So what did Grandma Tiny know that the rest of us don't? She knew something about human nature that's easy to forget. Deep down inside all of us is a desire to know and be known. We need people in our space who accept us, love us, and support us. Every person needs this, and the truth is, we can't live our lives without this dynamic. No one was created to walk life alone. Some of us may try to live this sort of lifestyle, detached from relationships and human contact, but the truth is we can't survive this way. If you try and live your life avoiding people, you will only survive for so long. Eventually, we get so messed up that we start talking to invisible people and repeating Third Eye Blind[34] lyrics as we roll around in our living rooms.

The more time we spend detached from others, the easier it is to live like we don't need people. The truth, however, is no matter how independent, resilient, or introverted we are, we all need one another. It's ingrained in our psyche to know and be known; we can't live life like the Lone Ranger.

In the beginning of Scripture's incredible narrative, God creates everything and decides from the get-go that is wasn't good for man to be alone. It's a pretty bold statement when you think about it. He designed us in His own image, and also declared it wasn't good for us to be alone. It shows God not only created community, but believes we need it. God eventually makes Adam's counterpart named Eve. When Adam sees her for the first time, he cries out, "This is bone of my bone, and flesh of my flesh."[35] His words are poetic. A light has turned on in his head, and he understands Eve will be his partner. Then, there is an interesting word used later on in the story. Most translations say Adam "made love" or "lay with his wife." We get what is being said here. The interesting thing, though, is the meaning of the Hebrew word. The word is *yada,* and it means, *to know.* Adam knows his wife and it is deep, beautiful, and sacred.

In the very next book of the Bible, Exodus, there is a beautiful exchange between God and one of the more formidable characters of the Old Testament, Moses. The conversation takes place after God has given Moses the Ten Commandments and has interacted with him on Mount Sinai. Moses begins asking God questions, trying to see if God is really going to be with Moses and not leave him alone. Essentially, Moses tells God, "If you go with me, I'll be fine; if you don't, I will not go." Then Moses prays with a high degree of audacity, asking God to show him His glory. God reassures Moses that He will indeed go with him because He knows Moses by name.

There is power in knowing someone by name, isn't there? Without knowing a name, someone or something is generic and confused with everything else.

My wife and I have this picture hanging in our bathroom of Audrey Hepburn. We bought it a few years ago and then took it to a local craft store to get a frame put on it. I'll never forget what happened when we went back to the store to pick up the picture. The guy who worked the frame counters couldn't find it anywhere. Panic set in. We thought they'd lost our beloved Audrey! We got a little irritated, but we tried our best to describe the picture in great detail. Finally, the manager came over and started to apologize, saying that this never happens and she would look for the painting. She asked what exactly was happening in the picture. We told her it was Audrey Hepburn with her hair up in a bun and a cigarette. She brought us a wrapped picture with the words "Smoking woman" written on the front. She opened it, and sure enough it was our picture.

We started laughing with the manager. The manager remarked, "Who doesn't recognize Audrey Hepburn?!" I felt like Audrey Hepburn was rolling in her grave to be described as "Smoking Woman."

Sometimes life can feel like that—like one long sequence of being forgotten. We ask ourselves constantly: Who really knows me? But to be called by name is a powerful thing. God says this is true about every one of us. We aren't merely "humans," but sons and daughters who our Father loves and is excited about. He knows us by name and calls to us sweetly.

Jesus came to show us how to truly know God and people. He instituted the church, a living, breathing community of people seeking to know and be known. The concept is quite extraordinary. God made a community to exist in this world to mirror the kind of closeness we will experience some day in Heaven. Furthermore, he created a family for those who have none. No matter what our life is like currently, there is a place for us to belong and to be known.

Grandma Tiny passed away about a year ago. Although she's gone, the lessons she taught through acceptance and love are still felt. She understood that the church is the greatest concept ever conceived. Her life communicated an incredible truth to everyone who came through the doors: This is a place to know and be known. We do our best to live with that kind of openness: to be a place where names are known and shared and where lives intersect.

Because we should never underestimate the power of community.

We should never forget the beauty of being known. Being known, after all, is yet another sign of living *in between.*

Unsurpassable Worth

God is in the people business. He sees beauty and worth in every person on this planet.

I have some friends who started an organization a few years ago called Povertees.[36] One night they sat around thinking about what they could do to love people and came up with this idea. They started spending time in downtown Los Angeles, hanging out and making friends with the homeless, a segment of society that is often ignored. Their idea was to make t-shirts with pockets on them and use the funds from the shirts to help feed people and lead them out of poverty.

The crew began by making shirts and heading to downtown LA to help people…but it transformed into something else. It wasn't just about making a shirt or even helping people; instead, it became about hanging out with their friends in LA. They made shirts so that their friends could eat; they raised money so opportunities could be created for their friends. This group became about loving people not because they were a project or even because Jesus would love them. Rather, their trips to LA, as well as their t-shirts, were made because they began living life together. And that is beautiful.

It's easy to forget that people have worth and value not because of what they do, but because they are human. God's image is in them. We call out this beauty when we love people not out of Christian service or ministry, but because we are people too. Similarly, we are nice to people not because being nice is what a Christian does, but because being nice is the human thing to do. That's what my friends at Povertees understand. There is a fire in their hearts to love and serve, founded in our shared humanity. They've discovered we have brothers and sisters everywhere.

It's always struck me as kind of odd that the church makes a huge push towards benevolence in terms of giving, but not in terms of receiving. We are fine with giving money and time to serve those in need, but how often do we receive these same people? Our churches give lots of money towards charitable organizations and hold giant serve days, but do our churches actually include the same people we so valiantly serve? If our hands are open to give and love, are they also open to hold and welcome that same person in our lives? Do we see unsurpassable worth in every human being on this planet?

I have a friend named Peter who lives in our city and comes to our church. Peter is a unique character, and sometimes it's hard to love him. He's spent the last few years of his life living on the streets and wrestling with the demons that come from that way of living. Moreover, Peter is known for talking out loud to himself, inexplicable irate outbursts, and a few other social faux pas. Honestly, numerous times during the week he causes a lot of stress for our church as we try to work with him and serve him, and he reacts poorly. Sometimes it's easy to overlook Peter. We think: "What does he have to offer God or our church? What can he actually do?" And the answer might surprise us. Perhaps he doesn't have anything to offer at all. And maybe that is his gift.

I can count on running into Peter multiple times a week. We sip coffee and munch on doughnuts. We talk in our church's kitchen as we look for some food to give him for the week. Our conversations are always the same—we talk about movies, old TV shows from the eighties and nineties, and superheroes. And the truth is, I don't always look forward to seeing Peter every week. But Peter, with all his idiosyncrasies, is wonderful. Sure, he has his issues. But so do I. We are in this life together. Peter has become my friend. Sometimes he calls me during the week at church to talk. Other times, he stops by, and I listen. I want him to know that I hear him and love him.

In the book of Isaiah, we get a glimpse of a coming time when things will be different. We are told nations won't rise against nations, and people will pound their swords into plowshares; lions will lie down with the lambs. It's a beautiful poetic description of something called the Messianic Age—a time of peace where justice will prevail. People will no longer make war against each other. Incongruous groups will unite together in fellowship, just like the lion and lamb. There is coming a day when God will abolish the superficial societal boundaries we've constructed. No longer will your income or talents define your worth. Together, as one family, we will be united.

The hints of this new age are spoken of throughout the Old Testament and into the New. Over and over again, we hear rumors of a time of when renewal is coming. We're told it is the Messiah who ushers in this new age of fellowship and solidarity. When he arrives, a new way to live and exist will come to fruition.

There is a compelling story in Luke 19 that illustrates this new age. Jesus meets a little man named Zacchaeus. From the start, we learn Zacchaeus is an eccentric fellow, who even goes climbing a tree to see Jesus. Zacchaeus is a tax collector, meaning his life has been a tad bit unethical since tax collectors were notorious for stealing money from people. But in meeting Jesus, he is transformed. His heart is changed, and he begins to give back the money he took from others. All of a sudden, the people that Zacchaeus overlooked in his lifetime begin to meet a new person. Zacchaeus makes the decision that he's never going back to the way he was before.

When Jesus sees Zacchaeus, he doesn't see a tax collector or a notorious sinner of ill repute. He simply sees a person whom God loves. This is why Jesus says to the crowd of religious sycophants nearby, "This man, too, is a child of Abraham." By calling him a child of Abraham, Jesus was saying that Zacchaeus was just as important to God as the people who claimed a special position with God based on their perceived moral standing. Zacchaeus mattered to God then and now. There are no such things as good people and bad people to Jesus. Just people.

Jesus began a revolution ushering in this Messianic Age. He created a new norm for God's people, one that wasn't built on bloodlines, but on Him. Jesus taught us that all people belong, because all people are part of God's family. We are in this life together because even though we come from different backgrounds, have different struggles, and look different, we have much in common. We share in our humanity. Brothers and sisters, mothers and fathers—we are family through and through.

This new humanity is manifested in the realization that God dwells among us and in us. Not just some of us, but all of us. We make friends on the basis of our unity, not diversity, because in God's eyes there is no difference.

I've always been fascinated by the amount of interactions in the Gospels where Jesus touches people. Jesus touches just about everyone. He holds little children; He embraces the sick and diseased; His cloak brushes up against a woman who's been bleeding for years. Numerous moments of teaching and miracles are preceded by Jesus touching people. Often times, we gloss over those kinds of nuances in the Scriptures. We disregard it; claim it's simply cultural. However, when we begin to pay attention to what Jesus does, we begin to see He was being intentional. Part of valuing people meant touching them. It meant showing them they mattered greatly to God. People are worthy of love, respect, and human touch. The more we lovingly hold one another, the more apparent it becomes that skin feels the same, regardless of whose it is. When we begin to realize this, and act on this realization, we begin to live out the Kingdom here on earth.

The Messianic Age is upon us now. Jesus ushered in an era of renewal. It was renewal with His ministry…renewal with His life…renewal with His teachings and miracles. As His followers, we should be actively seeking to break down what separates us from one another, whether it is class, education, race, or even sin. It's time we take our hands out of our pockets and begin to recognize the worth in one another. It's time we stop simply making friends and begin living with family. Let us allow others to recognize that worth in our lives, and we'll turn and do the same. Then a movement of Jesus will overpower a world addicted to competition and outdoing one another.

I had a professor in college named David Timms who believed competition was a result of the fall of humanity in Genesis.[37] It was an interesting thought to say the least, especially for someone who is fairly competitive. He believed that competition didn't exist in God's original creation. "There was no need for competition," he said, because "man and woman lived peacefully and perfectly with their Creator, secure in their identity in God." But after sin entered the world, competition began to rear its ugly head. Since the perfect state God created was broken, humanity's worth no longer came solely from God. They saw one another as obstacles to overcome. Adam and Eve turn against one another and start blaming each other for eating the fruit. Essentially, they try to "outdo" one another in the garden.

The rest of the story of Scripture is a glimpse at competition amongst humans. We try and outdo our brothers and sisters at everything. Kings go to war. Presidents campaign against one another. We try out for teams and promotions. I've often wondered would we have a more peaceful world if competition didn't exist? Jesus envisions a world without competition. It's a world where we don't have to worry about outdoing one another. There is no need to be better than someone else because God measures our worth not by how we compare to others, but based on who He is and our identity in Him.

Competition will eventually die completely. One day, when we are standing in the throne room of the King, we won't be competing any longer. No more will we boast of our goodness compared to our fellow brothers and sisters. None of that will matter in God's eyes.

No, we will simply fall to our knees, amazed by grace and love. We will truly get what Paul meant when he said there is no Jew or Greek, no slave or free.[38] We are just in Christ. Jesus is the first and last word in our lives, and we will stand in his presence united. Heaven will be full of family—brothers and sisters who look different than us, but share the beauty of our humanity.

Everyday an opportunity to know and be known exists in our lives. Family is everywhere. Unsurpassable worth exists on every corner of the planet. How are we going to partake in our common humanity with others? The time has come when lions should be lying down with lambs. A new age has dawned where the church should be the norm for society. It's time to throw open her doors and not only seek to serve our brothers and sisters, but be willing to welcome them into our midst. The day has come for us to live unified as family who embody unsurpassable worth.

I'm learning this world is one beautiful, extended family. People everywhere are worthy of love and respect. Let's see the unsurpassable worth in others and ourselves. When we do, there are echoes of Heaven among us. Another subtle reminder of being caught *in between.*

Love Like an MC

True love is more than intentions; it's about movement. Sometimes we need to fall in love with God again and again.

We used to have a kid in our youth group who lived on this quasi-urban farm. His name was Josh, and he lived only a few minutes outside of downtown Los Angeles, but his family had this huge chunk of land. They had animals too—dogs, cats, chickens, ducks, and geese. His white geese would run around his yard and sometimes attack his golden retriever. I'm not sure exactly what happened, but at some point in time, one of his geese died.

Josh was in middle school when all of this took place. At his school, there happened to be a pretty girl that liked him. In true Junior High fashion, Josh, wanting to show his lack of affection and disinterest in this girl, brought her a present one-day. He made her a necklace and presented it to her. Now, no one is sure exactly what he was thinking when he gave her this present. The necklace he made her was a gold chain attached to a goosefoot.

Yep. Josh made her a necklace out of a goosefoot from his dead goose. She, in turn, rejected the goosefoot because…well, it was a goosefoot on a gold chain. I've seen the actual necklace years later. It's real. It's weird. And it smells. I never knew the girl he gave the necklace to, but I can't help but wonder if something changed for her in that moment. She ran far, far away. Her love was rejected, and she has probably sought a lot of counseling since the fateful day.

My fear is that many of us have only encountered misrepresentations of God—where God is like a gift we don't want. We run away because someone has given us a description of God that isn't true or good or beautiful.

I remember the first time I said *yes* to Jesus and began to experience the gift of knowing Him. That might sound corny, but I remember being young and sitting in church thinking about this thing called faith. Before I got baptized, I sat in the pastor's office, and he asked me questions about God that I answered. I have no idea what my answers actually were, but I must have said something correctly because I got baptized soon after that. That was the start of my journey of faith; a journey that has taken me many different places learning what it means to follow Jesus. It's been a journey of learning to show love to those around me, as well as learning what it means to be loved.

I dated a girl in high school and college for a couple of years. It was one of those relationships that, at the time, was everything to me. Then in hindsight, you realize how much time and energy you wasted. I was thinking about this relationship one day, especially since so many of our students at church were dating. I remembered being young and naive, only eighteen, and believing I knew everything about the world around me. I had found a girl and was ready to love her with all that I had. Looking back, I actually had a lot of love to give, and I gave it freely. People used to say that I fell in love so easily, and I never understood what that meant until I was older.

So this girl and I would do all the things couples do in the movies. We had these epic goodbyes, talked on the phone for hours and hours, and planned our lives together. I remember making these vows to a person I thought I loved and cared about. My heart was given away like it was a free sample from Costco.

I think one of the problems with young love is that we don't understand the power of our words. Carelessly, we toss around words like "love "and "faithfulness," thinking it means something, like if we use words we've heard in love songs it somehow makes us resilient to the pressures of the world. We fail to realize that in reality our words are like knives, peeling away the layers of our soul.

One day this perfect relationship came crashing down. All of a sudden, everything that made sense in the past was gone. Both of us had lost one another and didn't have anything to say to redeem the relationship. I remember thinking differently about time when everything came to a halt. I saw years flash before my eyes. I saw the moments we had deeply treasured years earlier appear to be not that important. The memories that I thought would matter years down the road slowly and surely faded from my mind. I reminisced about the times I had been so upset or sad in this relationship and wondered, "Why?" I realized my life was bigger than this, and in the grand scheme of things, the relationship didn't matter the way I thought it did years before.

Life has a way of changing your perspective. Sometimes what we value changes in the blink of an eye. I wonder if that is part of God's partnership with us in this world. He works to reveal to us what matters and where we should place our hope and trust. It makes us think about the vows we make.

It was customary in Jewish weddings for the bride and groom to share vows or written commitments to one another. It was a way of stating before a community that they were promised to one another. This way, their words would be backed up by action.

When a young Jewish couple were arranged to be married, and the two came to the appropriate age, they would enter into a time of engagement for about a year. During this time, the future husband would go and prepare a place for his bride. He would build her a house. A house! Talk about a commitment. If he wanted her to be his bride, he would do the work and prepare their future dwellings. Then, in their wedding ceremony, they would recite promises. Essentially, part of his vow was that he had a place for her to come home to.

As I thought about this and the words and vows I had made in my life, I realized I had never been ready to build a house for someone. It wasn't until I met my wife that I realized the true meaning of making vows. It wasn't passive or forced. My vow was to be with her indefinitely— to hold her by my side forever. I promised to build her a house.

A relationship with Jesus feels a lot like wedding vows. In fact, knowing God in an intimate way is quite similar to a marriage. Scripture acts as His vow and also our wedding album. Over and over again, His words of commitment are spelled out to us. Visions of His faithfulness dance on the pages. He is a God who is for us and for all of time. He's been inviting us into a relationship. It is the proof that He is worthy of a commitment. I guess the question is, will we respond to His vows?

I went to a wedding once where the bride and groom wrote their own vows. This in and of itself doesn't seem like a big deal, but at this particular wedding, the couples' vows were night and day different. The groom began his vow by promising his bride that he would always make her soup. He followed up his promise with a story. When they were first dating, she went out of her way to care for him when he got sick. She brought him soup and because of her self-less act, he began to fall for her. So in front of family and friends, he vowed to honor and take care of his bride with the same passion and love that she had shown him.

The bride, on the other hand, promised to be faithful, just as he had been faithful to her. The couple had dated for a few years and had gone through a whirlwind of circumstances. They had gone through seasons of long-distance in their relationship, pursuing their respective careers, living in Los Angeles and New York. Furthermore, they had given each other the opportunity to pursue dreams, all the while supporting one another. And through all the changes and even the relational turmoil that was unleashed during their moments of separation, he had been faithful to her. She vowed the same.

I heard these vows, the beauty and honesty of them, and they shook me. I could tell these weren't cliché sayings stolen from Hallmark cards, but truth they had lived out. I knew this couple cared deeply about one another, and their marriage was built on a foundation of true love.

If you don't see your relationship with God like a marriage, maybe you should. See God as an intimate partner with whom you can share your life. Instead of God being some distant, removed figure, begin to live everyday like He is by your side, like you're living as a team. There is a difference after all between *knowing about God* and *knowing Him.*

Can you imagine a marriage where both parties claim knowledge about the other and that is the extent of their relationship? The husband knows facts about his wife, like her birthday and where she went to college. And she in turn knows stuff about her husband like where he works and what his favorite football team is. But we have to ask: Is that really knowing someone?

When we reduce God strictly to a set of principles and concepts, He is not the object of our love and affection, but merely a historical figure. He is in the same camp as George Washington. We brag about Washington's character and make jokes about his teeth and wig. But we haven't fallen in love with him.

Like a groom with fire in his eyes for his new bride, we haven't passionately said "yes" to God. We have ignored his invitation to walk down the aisle and make our vows to Him. Rather

than celebrate a lively relationship with the God of Heaven and
Earth, we have belabored facts about Him and become lost in a sea
of theological jargon. The clearest and simplest call to love Him has
been overshadowed by our attempts to know more about Him. And
He remains steadfast, asking us to walk with Him. He calls us to
stand at the altar and make our vow.

A couple years ago, I went to an underground hip-hop show in
Inglewood. I knew one of the performers that night from school, and
we'd even played some music together in the past. A friend and I
wandered around until we found the venue, which was in the
basement of a bar. The whole thing started late, around ten at night.
Once the doors opened, people filed into the bar, and the performers
took the stage. People stood around holding drinks in their hands and
swaying to the music. I'd been to a number of shows before, but this
one was different. I stared around the room, looking at different
people gathered around, waiting to hear from the various artists.

As people took the stage, I noticed something fascinating about
the experience. I've always loved music and enjoyed it, but there
was a different vibe in the air tonight. Hip-hop wasn't just another
genre of music here. It was life. It was fluid and moving, poetically
and beautifully connecting with the crowd. I like rap and hip-hop,
but this was more than just a casual recognition of something. The
artists here weren't on the radio or MTV. They rapped not for fame
or money or to prove they understood hip-hop, but because they
knew hip-hop—it had their hearts.

I have an extra large red t-shirt hanging in my office from this
show. It was thrown from the stage, and perhaps I looked pathetic or
like I didn't belong, or someone took pity on me. Whatever the
reasons, someone handed me the shirt. The shirt reads "MC Cali to
Worldwide." The shirt represents a movement, a story of love
between artists and their craft. I feel inspired when I look at the shirt.
I ask myself: Do I love God the way MC's love hip-hop? Do I love
the gift of being in a relationship with God the way these artists
loved their craft?

I think about that kid from our youth group who gave the girl a goosefoot necklace. I think about the times when I don't give God my best, when I play lip service to who He is and don't live a changed life giving Him honor and glory. I think back to those hip-hop artists. Am I sold out, not expecting anything out of the relationship? Do I realize that the gift of Jesus Christ is Jesus Christ? Can I make my vow based on that truth alone?

Sometimes we have to choose to fall in love with God all over again. Often times, couples will renew their vows after twenty or thirty years. The same is true for our relationship with God. Our vows to God are renewable. We renew our vows constantly, reminded of the love we have, and the gift it is to know God and be found in Him. We remind ourselves about what it means to make a vow to the God of Heaven and Earth, a truth we live with everyday; a truth that reminds us of *life in between.*

The Dance of Grace and Truth

Central to God's character are grace and truth. They are dance partners, interwoven into the fabric of living life in between.

A couple years ago, I was at an event Rob Bell and Cartlon Cuse put on in LA.[39] They were talking for a while about having a television show where they'd interview different people on spiritual topics. There was music, questions from the audience, and then Rob spoke. The whole thing was pretty wonderful, and Rob said something that night that stuck with me and has haunted me in a beautiful way ever since. He said, "Grace and truth are great dance partners."

Grace allows us to be open to receive; truth speaks to our soul. The pair are integral to our lives, and you can't have one without the other. Grace reminds us God is forgiving and kind; truth reminds us we are in desperate need of His love. Speaking of grace and truth like dance partners makes me wonder if God is like a good dance partner too. I wonder if He is waiting for us to answer His call and step onto the floor. Perhaps He reaches out and takes our hand and leads us in a waltz of the spirit.

A while back my wife and I used to take swing dance lessons at this little hole-in-the-wall club. The place was full of hepcats and elderly folks who were holding onto traditions from a time dead and gone. It was a blast.

The process was pretty straightforward. We'd show up, and two dance instructors taught us how to move our feet and what to do with our hands. We'd learn a new move and then switch partners, trying out said new move with a new partner. Then, after the lesson, we'd be given a chance to practice on the dance floor. People could always tell the beginners from the experts. The beginners were clumsy; the experts were fluid. The beginners had to stop and restart most times; the experts kept going and going. But there was really one factor that stood out—the beginners are learning how to lead and be led.

There was one guy who took lessons with us named Bob. He was the nicest guy you could ever meet, a real gentleman. But no one wanted to dance with Bob, and I knew secretly all the ladies prayed he wouldn't become their partner. I felt bad until I saw how often Bob stepped on feet. It was actually quite alarming. It happened so frequently that I wondered if Bob was a foot fetishist and swing dancing was his cover up for touching feet. He would do the same moves over and over again, all the while stepping on women's feet.

If a relationship with God is a dance, then it's a waltz of our soul interacting with Him, our will colliding with His. Often times it's messy. Back and forth, we jockey for position, stepping on God's feet because we haven't learned how to let Him lead yet.

It brings up an interesting question, though: are we being led or too busy trying to lead? I wonder if God is calling us to let go. He reminds us that to dance is to learn. He is teaching us how to be the soul we were created to be. If we listen closely, God is calling us to see with new eyes and hear with new ears, that we might be aware of living in between.

Henri Nouwen once said our greatest calling as leaders is to learn to think theologically.[40] Learning to think theologically has the potential to change everything. Essentially, we are asking God for a new perspective in which to view one another and the world. Thinking about life with this theological lens is not about getting trapped in an unending list of rules and regulations, squeezing the very essence out of life. Instead, it is about learning to see. Some of the most religious people are well trained in theology and biblical studies, and yet they don't know how to see.

The more we dance with God, the greater our trust in Him becomes. I have this feeling bubble up inside me when I realize He is someone I can trust. He sees people in ways I don't and has a perspective bigger, grander, and deeper than my own.

I love the conversion story of Paul in Acts 9. It's really a fascinating account of how God sees people. Paul, an enemy of the church, is rescued from his life of persecuting the church and becomes its leading apologist and missionary. Several chapters later, the tables have turned on Paul. Now he is the one being arrested by the people he used to work for. Talk about role reversal. I read this story of Paul, and it reminds me to have trust. In Paul, God didn't see an enemy or a threat to His Kingdom; rather, He saw the future voice of the church.

Having a reckless trust in God is faith in the midst of confusion. It's not about having the right answers, but walking through doubt and confusion, believing God will guide us to what is next. It's stepping on that dance floor. It's responding with our souls and hearts, not just our minds. If God saw Paul despite his rap sheet, I wonder how He sees us. Perhaps God is calling us to practice a little faith. He wants to guide us in an experience of grace and truth; He wants to teach us how to see and think differently in this world.

One of the primary pitfalls in our spiritual lives is that we often forget to trust God. Instead, we begin to test Him. In the book of Exodus, we have one of the clearest examples of God's heart towards His people. We learn in the Exodus account that our God hears the cries of afflictions and responds. The story of the Exodus resonates so strongly with Jewish people that even in this day and age, they still refer to the event as "when God led us out of Egypt." This story from so long ago is still their story.

After God saves his people from the clutches of Egypt, He leads them into the desert. He is a God who saves them and now provides for them. But an interesting thing happens by the time we reach Chapter 16 of Exodus. The Israelites begin to complain and quarrel to Moses that there is no food. So, Moses goes before God and asks for food. God provides manna and quail. The people eat and are nourished. He asks them not to gather more than they need. He's asking them to trust Him. But they don't. The Israelites gather their food for the day and grab extra for tomorrow. God causes the extra manna to spoil. And He's angry.

Next, God leads them to another place in the wilderness. Almost immediately, the Israelites complain that there is no water. Once again they quarrel and complain to Moses. And Moses says something interesting to them. He asks them why they are "testing the Lord." This place eventually is called Massah, which means a place of testing. After all God had done for His people—hearing their cries, delivering them from lives of slavery in Egypt, and crossing the Red Sea— they still are testing Him. Instead of trusting God, they try Him. Eventually, they even construct a false god to worship instead of Yahweh.

The gospel of Matthew goes to great lengths to paint a portrait of Jesus as God's true son—a true Israelite. Jesus' life mimics Israel's in a way. He, too, is delivered from Egypt as a baby. He is baptized, coming out of the water much like the Israelites are led through the Red Sea. He goes to the desert for forty days and nights; Israel wandered in the desert for forty years. And He is tested in the wilderness much like Israel (Matthew 4:1-11). Except Jesus doesn't test God. Instead, He trusts Him and is victorious whereas Israel failed. Jesus quotes three Scriptures from Deuteronomy during His testing in the desert; three Scriptures found in the story of Israel's desert wandering. After the testing, Jesus goes up a mountain like Moses and gives His law in a section of Scripture called the Sermon on the Mount (Matthew 5-7).

Perhaps Israel failed to trust God because they didn't have an example of what true faith looked like. They knew God's character and love, but they had failed to see it put in action. Jesus is our guide for trusting God. His reckless abandonment of Himself in order to serve is our example to imitate. The true Israelite is the one who does the Father's will. God is asking us to dance. He's extending His hand, hoping we'll accept the invitation. He shows us His son as an example of this trust, offering His Spirit in our lives to guide and protect us.

To dance with God is a process. It feels awkward at times. We wonder if we are learning to move with Him or if we're still stepping on His feet. His voice is telling us again and again to trust Him. When we wonder if we can trust, He asks us to turn our eyes to Jesus, our example in the faith. If we can stay close to Him, we will learn this dance God presents us with: a dance full of grace and truth.

All of this causes us to think about God's intentions for us. What is it He intends for His people? He intends good. God intends for us to live a life with grace and truth. We need grace for our lowest point, and truth to reveal Who and what is right. Jesus taught us this too.

Jesus led with grace and followed up with truth. Too often we do the opposite. We tend to make sure everyone knows the truth and try to show grace after the fact. Now, to be sure, God desires we know what is truth and what is not…but He also understands that we are fragile creatures in need of His grace.

John's gospel paints this picture quite clearly. In John 1:14, we read, "The Law came through Moses; grace and truth came through Jesus Christ." God was changing the scenery with the arrival of Christ. He was revealing what He intends for us. Remember the story of the woman caught in adultery in John 8? It's an odd story to be sure, but it seems to echo the statement of Jesus bringing grace and truth.

After this woman was brought before Jesus, He questions those so eager to condemn her. With a few simple questions and poignantly timed pauses, Jesus exposes their hypocrisy and calloused hearts, and they leave. Just the woman and Jesus remain. Jesus responds to her, "Does anyone condemn you?" She shakes her head no. "Then neither do I condemn you," He says. That is grace. He continues, "Now, go and leave your life of sin." And there's the truth. Jesus offers the same profound statements to us all. We are not condemned, but shown grace; and we are called to go live differently in truth.

Grace reminds us that God is for us, not against us. Truth reminds us that we are God's children in desperate need of His redemption.

Too often we talk about God in terms solely about what He's against. Being against something conjures up images of helplessness, as if God can't do anything but react. God is not a reactionary God though. He is a God who leads, creates, and inspires. Perhaps we should focus more on what He is *for* than what He is *against*.

Grace enables us to realize what God is for. Grace guides the way towards the heart of God. But so often, when we offer grace to others, it is limited. Our grace is selective. It operates on a whim, based on our feelings and our current disposition. We often show grace towards those we want to and harden our hearts to those whom we believe don't deserve grace. The problem, however, with selective grace is that it really isn't grace at all.

I heard a story once about man who had thirteen children. This man was sitting in his kitchen talking with a family friend. The friend asked him, "I know this is a weird question, but which one of your kids is your favorite?" The man paused at this question and began thinking over the answer in his head. Outside of the kitchen was one of this man's children, his youngest daughter, eagerly awaiting her father's response.

The man thought about it and then spoke. "Well, if I had to pick my favorite, it would probably be Shawn. I love his heart and enthusiasm." He paused and then began again. "But then again, I can't rule out Sandra. She is so intelligent and loves to learn. I love that about her. So, probably Sandra…And, yet, I can't forget about young Michael. He is a true leader in our family." The man went on to name each one of his children as his "favorite." What a perfect example of how our Heavenly Father operates for us. We are His children, His chosen ones.

God's thoughts are for us. His heart is open to all His children. His grace isn't selective, but all encompassing.

Typically, it seems, one of two things happen when people grow up in the church. The first route is one of self-righteousness. It's easy to head down this path. I know I have many times before. And I would be an egregious liar if I didn't admit to my own misgivings in the faith. This path develops a "better-than-you" attitude. And the interesting thing is that it's not always something we plan on doing. It just sort of happens. We become too "churchy," too "Christiany." Our world is the church, and it distorts our reality.

The other path is one of continued grace. I've met certain people who have been part of the church since they were young, kind of like that old saying—they were born on a Friday and in church on a Sunday. They've grown up in the faith, and yet they are still blown away by grace. They understand that grace is not a destination they reach one day, but a journey. Every day. Every year. They are learning more about the incredible grace given by our Father in Heaven—this Father who is crazy about loving people who don't deserve it.

The story of Heaven is really the story of unrequited love. Every person on this planet has experienced rejection. Even the most reticent of the bunch has mustered up some form of courage and approached a person we care for, only to have it slammed back in our face. There is a name for this—they call it junior high. With all kidding aside, though, rejection runs deep and gets progressively more serious as you get older. Rejection stings our souls. It reaches down into the very depths of who we are, and it breaks something special in us.

Unrequited love is this small voice that says, "You are not

good enough." And the truly despicable thing about the voice is that it repeats itself over and over again. If we hear it long enough, we may start to believe it. But then something beautiful happens— something surprising and unexpected. The unrequited love we experienced before begins to dissipate. We learn that someone else loves us. All of a sudden the loss and pain, the frustration and feelings of low-self esteem, are just a memory.

I imagine God is the ultimate beneficiary of unrequited love. Think of what we do and how we act. Imagine how our Father in Heaven must feel, how He must grieve when so many turn away from His open embrace. It's weird to think that I have grieved the Father. I've rejected Him on countless times. Nevertheless, this great God of Heaven and Earth keeps reaching out to me. He keeps telling me about this thing called *grace*. He whispers His message in my ear; He sings it to me in the early morning. At night, when darkness surrounds me and feelings of inadequacy and fear overwhelm me, He is present. Ever present. He is the ever-present God, existence itself. He's not leaving. Never. Ever.

As we mature in faith and life, we begin to learn that grace is a journey, not a destination. It's not a place we arrive at as if to say, "Here is grace. I've finally made it." It's not an age; it's not a feeling. Nor is it found in accomplishments. No, grace is at the beginning, the middle, and the end. It's a part of everything we do.

Every moment.
Every victory.
Every defeat.
Every triumph.
Every new beginning.

Grace is all around us. It is all encompassing and never-ending, and we belong to grace. We need to listen to that sweet voice. Let us open our eyes to see grace is all around and its never leaving. Let us embrace grace with all that we are because it is the only way we survive this ride.

When grace is no longer just a concept, but a lifestyle, we'll step back and see how different things are. When loving people unconditionally is natural because we, too, have been loved this way, we'll marvel at what God does in us. When we can fully accept grace in our own lives, it allows us to pass on grace to others.

I'll never forget my friend Gary that I met at Starbucks. I came across Gary, who was distraught and crestfallen. Life had not turned out the way he'd planned. We were complete strangers sitting across from one another sipping coffee. Gary overheard a conversation I was having with a friend and asked us if we were Christians. We replied, "yes," and he chuckled a bit, saying that he'd known Christians before, but he wasn't one anymore. Whenever I hear someone talk about Christianity, I'm always interested because it reveals something about their story and their perception of faith. I moved closer to Gary and listened to his story.

His life had been rife with struggles. Drugs, divorce, and rejection. He'd even been separated from his family, who were all back east. Something inside me was burning as Gary spoke, and I wanted to show him that following Jesus wasn't something legalistic or shallow. Eventually, he told us that he didn't' really like "church-people." I asked him what he meant by church people. He told me these were judgmental, close-minded people, people who had rejected him at his lowest point. I told him I didn't like those kinds of people either and what I was about was following Jesus.

As the conversation continued, Gary mentioned that he was far away from home. Normally in these kinds of circumstances, I'd pray for the person and then let him go on his way. But my friend and I didn't. Instead, we bought him a train ticket. Right then and there. Gary looked at us with tears in his eyes and thanked us. We were able to play a small part in reuniting Gary with his family. More importantly, though, we were able to share grace with Gary, the inescapable truth that his heavenly Father loved him dearly. We were able to remind him that grace is a journey, not a destination, and that we all need grace.

It was Frederick Buechner who once said, "Grace is something you can never get but can only be given. There's no way to earn it or deserve it or bring it about any more than you can deserve the taste of raspberries and cream or earn good looks or bring about your own birth."[41]

Grace is the ever-present, elusive truth that we are loved beyond measure, not because of what we do, but because of who God is. It's a journey of discovering and uncovering this truth in our lives. Moments appear where we can share this grace with others, revealing to us that we, too, have been given grace.

I'm learning to see every moment as an opportunity to experience God's grace both as I give it and receive it. It's a beautiful journey that we are walking together, moment by moment and grace by grace.

As Brenden Manning once said, "God loves us as we are, not as we ought to be. Because we will never be as we ought to be."[42]

Grace and truth are beautiful dance partners in this life of being caught *in between*. Grace leads us running back into our Father's arms. And truth allows us to be healed and set free. May we learn to see both as indispensable parts of our spiritual lives on our journey to God's heart.

Screenplays and Stories that Move Us

Story might be the greatest vehicle to teach us about God. Perhaps part of being a spiritually alive person is learning to live and think in narrative.

A while back I got pretty excited about screenwriting. Perhaps it was because I was living in LA, and everywhere I went I saw someone typing on a laptop, sipping an overpriced latte, and trying their best to make it. So, I decided to pursue my interest. I read books on film and screenwriting and even attended a seminar on "How to write for the movies" by renowned screenwriter Syd Field. I sat in an uncomfortable chair and listened to him lecture on the importance of literary structure and character development. I looked around the room and noticed I was literally surrounded by aspiring screenwriters who were working hard on their screenplays. Like me, they were hoping to get something out of the seminar to turn their aspirations into a reality. I took page after page of notes and realized even though I was learning about movies, I was also learning about life.

It just so happened that all of this was going on in a time in my life when I felt lost. There is a misconception out there that the longer you follow Jesus, the easier it becomes to not lose sight of Him. I guess I haven't found that truth. You can be actively attending a church, working at a church, and still forget your place in the story. It had been a few months since I felt God move in me. I was distant and closed off. I don't know if it was being bitter or dealing with the pain of what happens when expectations meet reality. But that was me. Instead of going to church, I went to a screenwriting seminar, and I heard God speak to me about my life.

Syd Field said that in screenwriting, the structure never changes. He called this the context. It's always the same. However, the content we form within the structure, now that is up to us. I thought about my context and content in my own life, and something inside me started to click. It was up to me to fill my context with the most beautiful content I could. What is beautiful content? I thought about my wife, family, friends, and my favorite movies. And I thought about the emptiness that we often wrestle with and how we're questioning what all of this is about. Some of us get caught thinking about a context when what we should really focus on is the content we place inside.

I have a life. My life isn't that different from the other billions of people on this planet. I rise and work, rest and sleep. I eat and drink; I laugh and play. I have twenty-four hours in my day just like every other person on planet Earth. There are many parts of my context I cannot control. Sure, I could make more money and live in another place, but my context still isn't that different from someone else's. What I can do, however, is choose how I fill my day. I can choose what story I tell within the context I've been given.

Later on in the workshop, we started talking about one of my favorite writers, F. Scott Fitzgerald. I've been somewhat enamored with him since I read the *Great Gatsby*[43] back in high school. He was a poet who knew how to turn a phrase and paint a tragically beautiful protagonist. He was also quite successful as a writer. When he grew older, though, he moved to Los Angeles to begin working on screenplays. Sadly, Fitzgerald died at young age before finishing his final book *The Great Tycoon.*[44]

He wrote screenplays and tried to make movies, but he failed at it. He failed miserably. No one would buy his scripts and screenplays. He slowly unraveled and eventually died from complications due to over-drinking. Ironically, in a town built on acting and the dramatic, his life unraveled rather plainly. One more drink, followed by another until it was too late. And the crazy thing is it's quite possible that F. Scott Fitzgerald died believing he was a failure. One of the greatest writers of the twentieth century died thinking he couldn't make it.

It's a sad, tragic story, isn't it? And it's all too familiar. In his song *Born and Raised* John Mayer has this great line where he sings, "I still have dreams, they're not the same, they don't fly as high as they used to." I interpret his lyrics to mean there is a progression we experience in life. As the years add up, we learn what content is most important for our lives. We never stop dreaming, but we do learn to frame those dreams in something greater than ourselves. I've noticed that the older I've gotten, the less self-centered my dreams have become. I find myself drawn to stories that call out the best in people and reflect sacrifice and love. The same themes separate the good and great stories.

I've always been a fan of stories, especially those told through film. Ever since I was young, I've been fascinated by the silver screen. I think my love of film began when I was in grade school. During the long summers in Oregon, I'd spend a significant amount of time at my uncle and aunt's house. They lived a few minutes outside of Portland, and their home was like Neverland. Not only did they have a giant pool in their backyard, but also a room full of movies my uncle would tape from TV. He was like the original pirate movie collector, a counterfeit Blockbuster. I also had a good childhood friend named Michael who lived next door. We'd spend long summer days swimming, playing basketball, and getting into whatever mischief we could muster up. It was the good life.

Every evening we'd hang out in the movie room. Michael and I would scan the black tapes, searching for adventure and intrigue. We'd find one whose title seemed interesting and pop it in the VCR. Hanging out in the den at my uncle's and aunt's was where I first saw *Star Wars, Indiana Jones*, and *Predator.*[45] I'd like to think in many ways that this was the place I discovered my sense of adventure—I know it's where I discovered my love of story. Long summer days ended sweetly, with the watching of movie after movie.

One of my favorite actors over the years has to be Audrey Hepburn. I watch her in a film and something inside screams out that this is what acting should be like. She has the ability to grab you from inside the movie and pull you into the scene. In fact, that's what good acting does. It causes you to believe. I like the movie *Breakfast at Tiffany's*[46] for that very reason. Audrey is believable. She lives alone in an apartment in New York with a nameless cat named "Cat." Her life is one big acting job. Her identity is intentionally covered by vagueness and intrigue about her past. As a viewer, you begin to fall in love with her the same way her male counterpart in the movie does.

Her performance not only commands your attention throughout the film, but in some weird, mystical way, reminds us that we, too, are searching for who we are. Good actors, and good movies for that matter, tend to speak truth into our lives. They deal with real issues that mean something to humanity, and cause us to deal with our own struggles. The human condition is brought to life in movies. We see our life on the screen in some way, shape, or form. We're able to say, "I get that. Me too." The story resonates with us. But it doesn't stop there. Good movies also give us a vision of a life different than the one we're living now. Truly great films connect with us at some point, but also inspire us for something better and bigger than our life at this moment.

Perhaps movies, then, are not only for entertainment purposes but also house the incredible ability to teach us. They teach us about the world we live in and the world that lives in each of us.

The first time I saw the film *American Beauty*[47] I was stunned. The movie is about a man going through a tragedian midlife crisis where he loses everything and finds everything at the same time. It's been called a modern retelling of the book of Ecclesiastes. I saw it with a friend at his house and I just sat on his couch for a good half a hour after the show, trying to interpret what just happened. The film spoke truth to me—truth that displayed different angles of life and what is important. I was struck by the observation that my life was full of meaninglessness gestures, desires, and pursuits. I was not just one character in the film, but a number of them. The film ends abruptly, showcasing the danger of meaninglessness. We are reminded a life built on meaninglessness is not life at all.

Any form of art has the potential to speak truth into our lives. Art, after all, is an expression of the human condition. It is our attempt to make something beautiful out of nothing. When Michelangelo carved his famous statue of David, he did it from a chunk of rock.[48] Andy Warhol started photographing and painting objects that seemed ordinary and boring like cans of soup and telephones.[49] How many songs have come from banging on a beat-up old guitar? How many stories have emerged from the tragedy of life and experiences we'd rather forget, and, yet, these memories fuel our imagination to tell beautiful stories? Art is not static and set; rather, it is alive and living in you and me.

Movies, like other forms of art, have the ability to teach us something about ourselves. They can carve away the stuff in the way and speak to us on a deeper level. Themes, hopes, and dreams come to the surface. Movies remind us that the process matters.

From the time we are little, people begin shoving scripts in our faces for us to live by. Be this; do this; go here and there. Time eventually sets us free to consider who we really are; that person we want to be. Our context is set. We live this life in this form from sunrise to sunset, but we have a choice on the content we produce. If life is an invitation to be who we were created to be, then why don't we see the potential we have for living beautifully and genuinely?

Jesus says in John 10 that He came to give us "life to the full." It's a phrase that reflects the eternal, carpe diem existence that Jesus talked about—an existence marked by love, altruism, justice, and acceptance. His claim on life, in many ways, mimics a conversation Moses has with the Israelites in the book of Deuteronomy.

After God has rescued His people and set them free from slavery, they've come to an impasse in the desert. Moses asks the people to make a decision. He says to them, "This day I call the heavens and the earth as witnesses against you that I have set before you life and death, blessings and curses. Now choose life, so that you and your children may live." (Deuteronomy 30:19, NIV)

The choice to choose life was before the Israelites. It was up to them to claim the life that was in front of them. The same choice is presented to us now. We have the choice to choose life.

I've learned from movies and screenwriting that characters are waiting to be guided to the next scene. In our own movie of our lives, do we guide ourselves forward? What script are we living by? Have we envisioned a life so compelling that it tells a captivating story in front of or behind the camera?

Screenwriting teaches us this life is about choices. Choose life and beauty; choose intrigue and passion. Choose to live a life of unparalleled adventure. Choose to exist and thrive *in between.*

The Truth Behind Fiction

The truth behind the stories we read and watch is that we are co-creators with God in this life. The pages are blank. It's up to us to write the story of our lives.

I'm not sure how it happened, but a few years ago, I found myself spending more of my reading time in the pages of fiction. That's how it used to be for me growing up. With book reports and reading logs due, I'd fill up the space with words from the *Boxcar Children*, and the *Hardy Boys*, and also those tantalizingly spooky *Goosebumps* books.[50] Seriously, how awesome were *Goosebumps?* Anyway, all of that changed by the time I reached high school. I became more interested in non-fiction, which I suppose is fine and all, but something inside me died when that happened. That sounds dramatic, but I believe it's true. Fiction and the power of story have the potential to breathe life into dry bones.

When I got back into fiction, I started to feel something again, something that had been gone for years. I felt creative. It was like that creative muscle went through atrophy after years of neglect. But now everything was different. I felt alive. I was flexing those creative muscles and slowly they were gaining strength. Fiction resurrected a part of me that had been in a deep slumber.

Growing up I had a love for stories. It was something my mind went to on walks home from school, or sitting in class, day dreaming instead of working on my fractions. When I was in middle school, our English teacher assigned a few stories for us to work on. I remember one was about an afternoon on the playground during recess. At that point in time, we were all playing football, so there were twenty stories or so about football. I always loved reading mine aloud. It was supposed to be written like a journalist, but mine was anything but that. It was completely biased, full of scathing remarks about the other team. I painted myself out to be the best wide receiver the playground ever witnessed. I was Jerry Rice in a Catholic school uniform.

During the same school year, we were assigned another story as well. This one was about a storm. I don't remember exactly why we needed to write about a storm, but every one in the class had to write three pages on a storm that came crashing down and what happened after the storm passed. One of my main characters was a cow named Bertha. After the storm destroyed everything, all that was left was Bertha, the cow, and myself. The story ended with me eating Bertha. It was really tragic stuff.

It was around that same time I decided to write my first story. I remember it like it was yesterday. I was in middle school, and I wanted to be a writer, so I began working on a concept that I thought would prove to be a bestseller. I started to write a story about a rogue fighter pilot inspired, in part I think, by watching *Top Gun*.[51] I wrote one page in a notebook. I introduced my main character, and I was excited to read about what happened next. The only problem was that starting the story meant I had to actually sit down and write it. Which never happened. But that was my first story—a one page, four paragraph introduction that never made it past the first page. My writing notebook was full of blank pages.

If we compare this life to a story, then our lives are sort of like blank pages. God has given us the pen and told us to write a story. He's watching us, waiting with us, walking with us, seeing what direction we may take our life. The problem is, many of us feel like we can't get past that first page. We're stuck. We have an infinitely creative God who made a world of beauty and intrigue, and we're stuck on the couch, in front of the television. Our stories turned into boring monologues about unrequited dreams and unlived potential.

The real storytellers are the ones who are brave enough to face the possibility of failure. They understand full well that writing the story is not always easy or fun, but it is the most beautiful calling one could have. Putting words on paper, like putting meaning in our lives, requires us to get outside of ourselves. It calls us to come forward in the morning and welcome in the sunrise, to be all that God created us to be regardless of what the world around us has to say about our choices. We run onwards to the future with strength, fortitude, and determination because that is our only choice. Writing is a burden, but it's also freedom. It's the freedom to create and share truth that comes to us in a variety of ways, especially in story.

The longer I study story, the more aware I am that we are structured to hear and tell and think in narrative. It has nothing to do with being right-brain versus left-brain dominant or having a love for books and movies. It simply has to do with being human.

The whole thing reminds me of that incredible character from the *Catcher in the Rye*—Holden Caulfield.[52] He's a grumpy, narcissistic, broken, and despondent teenager. We've all been there at one point or another in our lives. Adolescence is a rough time for everyone, and Holden represents the age brilliantly. Except there is more to it than that. Deep down inside the recesses and synapses of our existence, there is part of us that is like Holden. There is a place where we fear, loathe, hate, and are genuinely scared of what tomorrow might bring. When J.D. Salinger created the character, I don't know what his thought process was at the time. But I imagine he was reaching deep down into his inner life, and he brought forth a character that has been resonating with people for years.

Stories are powerful like that. They share with us a world that we know in our hearts. Stories speak the truth we long to hear, but have trouble articulating. Good stories do that. No matter the content, good stories reveal truths we can't ignore.

It's interesting how a good narrative has the power to change us. I think back to all the books and movies that have impacted my life. There are images and characters that I will never forget—some for their beauty and brilliance; others for their notoriety and evil. Fiction and stories tell us about the nature of life—both the seen and unseen. It's true that each one of us has a hidden life—a part of themselves that is not visible to the world around them. It contains our dreams and wishes concealed by day jobs and friendships. Or it could be secret passions that are overshadowed by voices of negativity and judgment. The hidden life is that true, deep, beautiful, sacred part of us that reveals who we really are. The inner self is brought to the surface when we engage good stories. Furthermore, good artists and authors know how to tap into theirs. That deep, mystical part of us knows when someone is speaking to it. So we respond accordingly.

God cares about stories too. Judaism and Christianity are overwhelmingly structured on narrative. That's basically the Bible in a nutshell. History, poetry, law, epistles, and wisdom literature are structured in the framework of narrative for the most part. If God gives us His word in the form of narrative, then there is something about stories that bring us closer to God. It's like the more we read, the closer we are getting to God's heart. He is the Inventor of story after all. When we share in good stories, we are sharing the heart of God.

Those of us who choose to bring forth stories have a role to play as well. We are the mouthpieces, the conduits of the creative energetic force that is narrative. The life of a writer is one of receiving and giving. We fill up so that we can share. Creative's have an important role to play in all this. There is a calling to fulfill.

The choice of intentionally writing one's life is really the life of a prophet. It requires one to strip himself of all titles and formalities and embrace a calling; a life of service to one's fellow man. We prepare to write our stories early, everyday, before time has its way with us. We face the morning, prepared to do battle. This is our calling. Like the biblical prophets of old, we face the crowds head on. We hear their rejections and complaints. We dodge the stones that fly from their hands. There exists an understanding that part of our calling requires facing fear and overcoming death's blow. This is the life we're called to lead.

Being a storyteller, is also about learning to see with new eyes and listen with new ears. The world is spinning in and out of control, and we find our place in the chaos and the noise. We find steadier footing where others feared to tread. It comes with the territory. It scares us, but that's half the fun of it really. There are times when it's kind of inspiring to do the impossible. When you really think about it, the whole writing thing is not about our ability. There is another force at work. Writers learn to trust in a higher power.

The best writing seems to happen in that weird place between full comprehension and daydreaming. I don't know if there is another way of phrasing it actually. It's like we are present and engaged, but our minds are elsewhere. It's tapped into an alternate reality where dreams coalesce and reality slips away. We spend whatever time we're granted in this zone and then come out of it. Down on the page in front of us are words, sentences, ideas, concepts, and characters all leaping off the page. And we begin to think, "I don't remember writing that or know where it came from." It's the beauty of writing. It's the calling of the prophet—we're given a word and now we must share it. It's not our word, but the One who gave it to us.

I've always loved the concept of each person having a genius. The Romans believed all creativity and inspiration came from a source. It wasn't us. It was outside of us, and we were responsible for being ready for our genius to appear. A person did their part, and then their genius did its. We just needed to show up, and the rest would take care of itself. I've felt that kind of incredible connection before, and I wasn't sure what to do with it other than let the words dance on the page in front of me and go from there.

There is truth in fiction because all fiction comes from a sacred place, a genius, spoken through a prophet. That's why we should love books and read them often, holding onto them regardless of what happens. Because there are ideas that need to shared. There are worlds that need to be created. There is salvation that needs to come to us through stories, the very way God intended it to be. So write your story. Live in your fiction. Because you aren't just writing nonsense. You are sharing gospel. Perhaps getting lost in story is about hearing the echoes of Heaven. It's about being *caught in between.*

Going Home

If we're all eventually passing through, perhaps we'd do well to pay attention to the way. The journey to get there starts here. One day, we are all going home.

I've always wondered if Heaven will feel familiar. When we arrive, will it be like walking down a familiar street or eating at our favorite restaurant. I'm not sure, of course, but I can't imagine it feeling foreign. When we get there, I don't envision needing a tour. I doubt Saint Peter is standing at the gates with a clipboard and a Double Decker Red Bus, instructing us to board for the four o'clock sight seeing tour. No, I imagine Heaven is familiar. Instead of feeling lost, we recognize the sights and sounds. It will feel like going home.

There was a sweet lady who lived at a retirement home nearby our church. Her name was Thelma. About once a month, I'd go to a special Sunday afternoon service at this retirement home. About ten or twelve residents would gather in a TV room to have church. We'd play hymns on the piano, share a brief message, and take communion together. It started at three o'clock in the afternoon. Usually, I was exhausted by that time of the day, so getting there was always tough. But, like most things, once I was there, I was glad I came.

The same residents showed up week after week. It was always a special time with lots of singing and laughing. I loved listening to one resident named Bob sing *How Great Thou Art.*[53] He only knew the chorus, you know the "How Great Thou Art" part, so he'd belt it out every time, right on cue and right on pitch. He really knew how to hit that one note. He did it so forcibly the first time that I jumped in my chair. The place was full of great characters like that. Thelma was one of them.

Thelma was a sweet lady in her eighties who wore sweaters and a matching knit hat, no matter the weather outside. With coke bottle glasses, deep dark eyes, and her hair perfectly straight, she peered up at you as she sat in her wheelchair and smiled in a polite sort of way. No matter how good or bad the singing was, or how the message went for that matter, she was glad to be there. I don't know how she did it, but Thelma held the group together. I heard her say the same phrase at least two dozen times in the span of a few years. Every person in the group would get a graceful hand on their shoulder and Thelma would simply say, "Jesus loves you. I love you. And that is all that matters." She said that to me a few times, and I believed her. Those words were rich and life giving. I looked forward to the gathering just to be near her and see her polite smile.

I remember one day I showed up, and Thelma wasn't there. Immediately, I knew why. She had never missed a Sunday afternoon church service in the couple of years I'd been attending. One of the residents soon confirmed what I knew: she had passed away. I left that day with an ache in my heart. Death is like that, even for someone who has lived a long, full life. Death is welcomed but never fully understood.

We used to have a kid who came to our youth group named Jared. He was a little rough around the edges—foul mouthed, rebellious towards authority, and a real smart aleck. I liked him a lot. He'd always come to youth group early so that he could play basketball in the gym. Often times on Wednesdays, we'd be shooting hoops for around an hour or so. Our games ranged from "Horse" to the "Around the World," but always found their way to a game of one-on-one. I loved shooting hoops with Jared. We didn't say much. Every once in a while we'd talk about life, high school, and God. Jared made me laugh every week. During our youth service, I could always count on him to participate in whatever game or challenge we had. I could also count on him to make the perfectly timed inappropriate comment. Every youth group needs a Jared. Eventually, Jared and his family moved out of California, and I didn't hear from him for the longest time.

One day we got news that Jared was in a car accident. He was still in high school when he died. A lot of our kids remembered Jared. They were friends. They were struck with a concrete example of how fragile and unpredictable life is. A number of our students attended his funeral that was held back in California. I remember thinking about Jared. I missed this rambunctious, foul-mouthed kid that played basketball with me before youth group. And I wasn't the only one. I remember logging onto MySpace (back when it existed). Jared's page was still up and was filled with comments from classmates and friends. I'd never seen anything like it before.

People left messages saying how they missed him or how he was special in their life. But there were a few messages I didn't expect to see. Some of the comments were by people who knew of Jared but didn't know him. They said things like " You seemed cool; I wish I would have talked to you more." Or, "We had English together. We didn't talk or anything, I wish we would have. I hope you're doing alright now." The condolences and comments went on for page after page. I read those comments with the familiar ache in my heart.

I've always wondered if God becomes a little jealous that certain individuals are on Earth and not in Heaven. This jealously can't stand the separation, so they get called home a little sooner. A good-hearted lady like Thelma is now at home, offering her encouragement and love in new beautiful ways. I bet she still makes it to service on time. And an energetic kid who loved basketball is making new friends and spewing plenty of smart aleck comments. I bet they love that stuff up there.

I remember hearing a Ben Franklin quote when I was younger. You know, the one where he says the only thing that is certain is death and taxes.[54] The part about taxes didn't make sense until I was older and had to pay them, but death always made sense. I guess that's because it came about fairly early in my life. I knew people who went to the other side when I was still a child. I learned from a young age that death was swift and unbiased. Its cold touch was all too familiar.

You see, my dad passed away when I was about four years old. Of course, I don't remember him. There are no memories, just fuzzy pictures that collected in my mind. Part of me thinks they're real; another part believes I made them up to have some recollection of from where I came. I can't be sure of course, but those memories are comforting even to this day. My dad passed away in the fall when the leaves begin to change color.

Although I didn't know much about my dad, I do know he was a fighter. My dad fought cancer for ten years. Ten years. He gave it his all for as long as he could. Later on, my aunt told me when it came close to the end, she leaned over his hospital bed and told him that it was okay, that he didn't have to fight any longer. It wasn't too long after that moment that the cancer won, as it usually does.

The event tore my family apart. We all struggled. We all mourned. Those were dark days. The whole thing weighed particularly hard on my grandpa, I'm told. Seeing his child suffer and die was too much for him. About a year later, my grandpa joined my dad, passing away the next fall. The coroners report said the cause of death was a heart attack, but my aunt held that he died of a broken heart. Losing his only son was too much to bear.

Death came quickly in my family, picking off the men one by one. But my grandma stood tall through everything, remaining steadfast. She lived another fifteen years on her own before it took her too.

The day my grandma passed away, she called me on the phone. I was in college in Southern California, and she was up north living in the Bay area. I didn't have a chance to see her, but I heard her voice on the phone. Her last words to me were to finish school and do well. My heart broke in that moment. Everything around me went dark. I remember sitting on my bed and crying, knowing that I would never see her again.

Whenever we're forced to say goodbye, there is a part of us that breaks. Saying goodbye for the last time on this earth is never easy. It takes courage and strength not only to say the words, but to go on living after the person has passed on. Sometimes it seems easier to skip saying goodbye. We shy away from it because we believe it means the end or a conclusion of something good. But this is not true. We should never shy away from it. Because in saying goodbye, we are releasing someone to the next great adventure. People need to know that we are okay. People need to know that we can let them go. People need to know that we're prepared to let them go home.

Death is not the end of the story. Death is not the conclusion. It is merely a transition to what's next. Life doesn't stop when someone is buried in the ground. In fact, some might even argue that life is really just starting. And I'm not talking necessarily about Heaven.

Although there are different views on what happens when someone dies, we have to continually approach the subject with openness and curiosity. Is there a Heaven? What about a Hell? Do ghosts and spirits walk around freely when the curtain is pulled over them? We can speculate all we want, but none of us is entirely sure. That's the trouble with death—no one has been able to go there and come back to tell us exactly what happens.

Regardless of what you think about Heaven and the afterlife, all of us can agree that the next phase, whatever it may be, is full of possibilities. We shouldn't fret or worry about the unknown. Rather, we should cling to it and embrace it. We must accept the mystery and the unknown, aware that just as this life brought moments of beauty and intrigue, the next life holds the same.

This is why saying goodbye is a vital discipline for our lives. It takes courage and strength to say those words and to go on living when someone you cared about is gone. Life is full of those moments where we say goodbye and move on towards something else. But in moving on, we aren't diminishing the significance or importance of what took place before. Instead, we are releasing that person to exist in another way. This is why memories are so important. They call us to embrace life. They invite us to travel back in time to the way things were. Even in dying, they remind us of what was and what is.

Death never feels timely. But it also never feels final. I love when Jesus says in the scriptures that He is going to prepare a place for us. In John 14:2, Jesus says that His "Father's house has many rooms." It's a sprawling mansion with room enough for all. He also says that Heaven is like a wedding feast with plenty of room at His table.[55] It's a mansion. It's a feast. This means Heaven is full of merriment and partying, like one giant family reunion. Death doesn't seem as scary when we realize that we're not saying goodbye; instead, we're just going home.

I think about my dad and grandparents often. I close my eyes and see them. I think about Thelma and Jared too, and I know they've all gone home. After a long journey, nothing is better than finally getting back to where you belong. It's good to go home.

If Heaven turns out to be familiar, then the transition from here to there will be a natural one. It will be like waking up from a deep slumber and welcoming the morning with open arms. The coffee is hot and fresh, and the newspaper is on your porch. You have the sensation that something is slightly different but not in a bad way. It's as if Heaven is your true home.

It's all too easy to take time for granted. I wish I could choose how I'm going to die. I'd tell God to make me old and grey, full of years. I want to see how big my nose and ears will get if I live to a hundred. I want to have one final party. I want to eat my wife's cooking one last time. Then I can go. Then I will greet Heaven with open arms.

The truth is, we don't get to decide those sorts of things. All we can do is live now like we are going to live there. And realize that when our number is called, we are just going home.

This life is a beautiful gift, but it's also merely a shadow of what is to come. German theologian Augustus Crusius was on his deathbed when he said, "My soul is full of the mercy of Jesus Christ. My whole soul is towards God." That's someone who knows they are going home. It's the perspective that what is here is connected to what is to come. Jesus spoke a lot about "eternal life" in the Scriptures, particularly in the gospel of John. The phrase eternal life in Greek is *zoe aionios.*[56] Scholars translate it as *eternal life*, *life to the full*, and *life of the ages.*

John says eternal life is tantamount to knowing Jesus. If you know Jesus, then you are experiencing the best life possible. I love that. The few pictures we have of Heaven in the Scriptures describe it as a joyous gathering where we are united with God in a state of rapturous delight. It's our true home that is peeking through the veil. It's why we can describe moments in this life as "other worldly." It's as if something deeper and more beautiful is slipping through, like Heaven is seeping through to Earth.

Death will continue to cause us confusion and pain. When we say goodbye in this life, it's never easy. We're never prepared for this life to end. The tears will fall, and our hearts will rightly ache. We'll find ourselves missing those who have gone on to what is next. However, we'll also be filled with joy knowing this is not the end.

One day we too will go home and see those who have gone on before us. When we make the journey from here to there, from one home to our true home, Jesus will welcome us in. He'll extend a seat to us at the banquet table. He'll hand us a key to a room in His innumerable mansion. We'll laugh and cry, waking up to what is familiar. And we'll smile because we've gone home to the place He's been preparing for us. We'll discover what we've known all along—that we were *caught in between* and now we've arrived.

A Final Word

You and I are part of a new land. We are embarking in new territory, the New Jerusalem. Brothers. Sisters. Mothers. Fathers. This new land is family. We are refined by Holy fire as we prepare for the great wedding feast. The Hound of Heaven is ruthless in His pursuit of His bride. He will stop at nothing to make preparations for our arrival. Our homecoming is signaled by a heavenly chorus, celebrating uproariously as one more lost soul finds its home. But we should not forget this life is not without struggle.

We're being tested everyday. Conflict is necessary for our growth. Pain and suffering are but birth pains, subtle reminders of passing from one life to the next. Our rebirth is the freedom to no longer live as the world does, but to choose to see this life for what it really is—reflecting the beauty of the world that is and is coming. Our temporary home can take what it wants. We surrender ourselves over to its demands realizing that every day we are getting closer to life.

We strive and fight, struggling for our glorious future. Instead of sitting idly by watching the world pass on, we embrace all that has been given to us. The sun, the moon, and the planets rejoice with us. As Paul said, we are learning what it means to be "more than conquerors."[57] We are more than warriors crossing enemy lines. We are royalty, rightly claiming our place in the King's throne room. The lies of this world are fading; no longer do they entrap us. We've found our sanctuary.

This is what it means to live life *in between*. We are homesick for a place we've never been, but the time is closer now than ever before. This is what it means to see your story connected to the grand narrative of the universe. More is happening in us and around us than we ever realized.

There is more to say and so much more to learn. We're barely turning the page on this story, but it's becoming clearer every day. Together we strive for what we know to be true. Faith, after all, is the hope and certainty of what we do not see. What we didn't know before, though, was that not seeing was really another way of seeing. Clarity is unfolding as we strive forward.

May you come to see your own story as something beautiful and radiant; may you come to see yourself as *caught in between*.

The Acknowledgements

There are several people I need to thank for helping me put this book together.

Kyle, thank you for reading this manuscript and editing it. I couldn't have done it without you. I learned a ton from you during this process and I'm so incredibly thankful for your friendship. Love you dude!

Kelly, thank you for helping me not only edit the book, but learn the ins and outs of formatting it.

Paul, thank you for creating the perfect cover. You captured the essence of the book with your incredible art.

Downey First, thank you for being an unbelievable community. I'm so thankful for your guidance, support, and love over the years. Thank you for showing me Jesus.

Marissa, thank you for your constant support over the years. You've read so many of my books and blog posts and are constantly encouraging me. I'm so thankful to live this life with you. Thank you for loving me and inspiring me to be a better person. I love you.

Uncle Martin, I wish you could have read this before you went storming through those pearly gates. No longer are you caught in between; now, you're fully there. Thank you for being family, even when you didn't have to be. I'm eternally grateful for the gift of knowing you.

The Notes

---

[1] This quote, of course, is from Braveheart—aka copious amounts of blue paint and Scottish kilts. <u>Braveheart.</u> Dir. Mel Gibson. Paramount Pictures, 1995.

[2] Perry, Katy. <u>Teenage Dream.</u> Capitol Records, 2010

[3] Pascal, Blaise. <u>Pensees</u> Penguin Classics: New York, 1995

[4] Acts 2:17-21

[5] Chbosky, Stephen. <u>The Perks of Being a Wallflower.</u> Pocket Books: New York, 1999. Go ahead and read this book. You'll be glad you did.

[6] Hebrews 6:19

[7] Kerouac, Jack <u>On the Road.</u> Viking Press: New York, 1957. If you didn't read this book in High School English, check it out. Scratch that. Even if you did, read it again.

[8] Luke 24:13-35

[9] Homer, <u>Odyssey</u>. Cambridge: Harvard UP, 1995. Print.

[10] Tolkien, J. R. R. <u>The Hobbit</u>. 1937 George Allen and Unwin: UK, 1937

[11] Rowling, J. K. <u>Harry Potter and the Sorcerer's Stone</u> Bloomsbury: UK, 1997. Okay, if you haven't read Harry Potter yet, just do it...like right now...or we can't be friends.

[12] Frost, Robert. <u>The Road Not Taken</u> Henry Holt and Company: New York, 1920.

[13] <u>Boyhood</u>. Dir. Richard Linklater. Universal Pictures, 2014

[14] Rice, Damien. <u>Cannonball.</u> Rathgar and Celbridge: Dublin, 2002

[15] Miller, Donald <u>A Million Miles in a Thousand Years.</u> Thomas Nelson, 2009.

[16] The story is told in Joshua 3-4

[17] John Lennon is quoted saying this on the recording of his song, "Beautiful Boy." Lennon, John. <u>Beautiful Boy</u>. Geffen Records, 1981.

[18] <u>The Great Dictator.</u> Dir. Charlie Chaplin. Criterion Collection, 1940.

[19] This is from the book Orthodoxy. Chesterton, G. K. <u>Orthodoxy</u>. Dodd, Mead and Company, 1908.

[20] <u>The Graduate.</u> Dir. Mike Nichols. United Artists, 1967

[21] Keller, Helen <u>The Open Door.</u> Doubleday & Co, 1957. But seriously. How good is this quote?!

[22] The greatest commandment question is from Luke 10:25-28

[23] Deuteronomy 6:4-9

[24] Listening and reading anything by Rob Bell over the years taught me so much about the context of the first century. His explanation of rabbis and the rabbinical way of life is incredible.

[25] These movies are too good. Bye Felicia. <u>Friday.</u> Dir. F. Gary Gary, Steve Carr, and Marcus Raboy. New Line Cinema, 1995.

[26] Can't Buy Me Love. Dir. Steve Rash Buena Vista Pictures, 1987

[27] Nouwen, Henri J.M. The Return of the Prodigal Son: A Story of Homecoming Doubleday, 1994

[28] Sabrina Dir. Billy Wilder. Paramount Pictures, 1954

[29] Luke 14

[30] Matthew 22:14

[31] Stott, John. The Letters of John. Tyndale New Testament Commentaries, 2009

[32] Oh professional wrestling. So fun. So ridiculous. So fake. The Rock and Bret Micahels were staples of this industry. Google, my friends. Just google.

[33] The Sermon on the Mount is found in Matthew 5-7.

[34] I love Third Eye Blind. No offense to them, but their songs do get stuck in your head…forever…

[35] Genesis 2:23

[36] Please check them out. The work they're doing is incredible—www.povertees.com

[37] Timms, David. Spiritual Leadership Residency. 12 January 2010. Also, check out any and all of his books.

[38] Galatians 3:28

[39] Rob Bell is one of my favorite authors and communicators. Carlton Cuse makes really cool television shows. Look them up.

[40] This comes from an incredible book on Christian Leadership

called "In the Name of Jesus." Nouwen, Henry <u>In the Name of Jesus</u> Crossroad Publishing Company, 1992

[41] Buechner, Frederick. <u>Wishful Thinking: A Seeker's ABC</u> Harper One, 1993

[42] Manning, Brennan. <u>The Ragamuffin Gospel</u> Multnomah, 2005

[43] To this day, this is still one of my favorite books. Fitzgerald, Scott <u>The Great Gatsby</u>. New York: Scribner, 1995

[44] Literally the book stops right in the middle. Still worth a read though. Fitzgerald, Scott <u>The Last Tycoon</u> New York: Scribner, 1941

[45] <u>Star Wars.</u> Dir. George Lucas Lucasfilms ltd, 1977. <u>Indiana Jones</u>. Dir. Steven Spielberg Paramount Pictures, 1981. <u>Predator</u> Dir. John McTieran 20th Century Fox, 1987

[46] <u>Breakfast at Tiffany's</u> Dir. Blake Edwards Paramount Pictures, 1961

[47] You should definitely see this movie. <u>American Beauty.</u> Dir. Sam Mendes Dreamworks Pictures, 1999

[48] I saw the real David statue in Florence. There are no words.

[49] Life goal: own an original Andy Warhol.

[50] All fantastic books from my childhood. Thank you, Franklin W. Dixon, Gertrude Chandler Warner, and R.L. Stine.

[51] Sing it with me now—"Highway to the Danger Zone!" I still think it's one of Tom Cruise's best films. <u>Top Gun.</u> Dir. Tony Scott Paramount Pictures, 1986

[52] Holden is one of my favorite characters in all of literature.

Salinger, J.D. The Catcher in the Rye Little, Brown and Company, 1951

[53] Remember when churches used to argue about whether to sing hymns or not? Awe, those were the good ol' days. How Great Thou Art written by Carl Gustav Boberg

[54] The actual quote: "In this world nothing can be said to be certain, except death and taxes." Benjamin Franklin

[55] Matthew 22

[56] Strong's Greek 2222 and Strong's Greek 166. Take out the old lexicon and look it up.

[57] Romans 8:37

Stephen Pate is a pastor and writer. He lives in Southern California. You can find out more about his writing and ministry by visiting www.stephenpate.org